ORPHEUS DESCENDING

with

BATTLE OF ANGELS

By TENNESSEE WILLIAMS

PLAYS

Cat on a Hot Tin Roof

The Glass Menagerie

27 Wagons Full of Cotton and Other Plays

A Streetcar Named Desire

Summer and Smoke

The Rose Tattoo

Camino Real

You Touched Me (with Donald Windham)

Baby Doll (a screenplay)

POETRY

Five Young American Poets, 1944

In the Winter of Cities

PROSE

The Roman Spring of Mrs. Stone

One Arm and Other Stories

Hard Candy and Other Stories

ORPHEUS DESCENDING

with

BATTLE OF ANGELS

Two Plays by TENNESSEE WILLIAMS

A NEW DIRECTIONS BOOK

Grateful acknowledgment is made to the New York *Times* in which the article "The Past, the Present and the Perhaps" first appeared.

For Marion Black Vaccaro

CONTENTS

THE PAST, THE PRESENT
AND THE PERHAPS

One icy bright winter morning in the last week of 1940, my brave representative, Audrey Wood, and I were crossing the Common in Boston, from an undistinguished hotel on one side to the grandeur of the Ritz-Carlton on the other. We had just read the morning notices of *Battle of Angels,* which had opened at the Wilbur the evening before. As we crossed the Common there was a series of loud reports like gunfire from the street that we were approaching, and one of us said, "My God, they're shooting at us!"

We were still laughing, a bit hysterically, as we entered the Ritz-Carlton suite in which the big brass of the Theatre Guild and director Margaret Webster were waiting for us with that special air of gentle gravity that hangs over the demise of a play so much like the atmosphere that hangs over a home from which a living soul has been snatched by the Reaper.

Not present was little Miriam Hopkins, who was understandably shattered and cloistered after the events of the evening before, in which a simulated on-stage fire had erupted clouds of smoke so realistically over both stage and auditorium that a lot of Theatre Guild first-nighters had fled choking from the Wilbur before the choking star took her bows, which were about the quickest and most distracted that I have seen in a theatre.

It was not that morning that I was informed that the show must close. That morning I was only told that the play must be cut to the bone. I came with a rewrite of the final scene and I remember saying, heroically, "I will crawl on my belly through brimstone if you will substitute this!" The response was gently evasive. It was a few mornings later that I received the *coup de grace,* the announcement that the play would close at the completion of its run in Boston. On that occasion I made an equally dramatic statement, on a note of anguish. "You don't seem to see that I put my heart into this play!"

It was Miss Webster who answered with a remark I have never forgotten and yet never heeded. She said, "You must not wear your heart on your sleeve for daws to peck at!" Someone else said, "At least you are not out of pocket." I don't think I had any answer for that one, any more than I had anything in my pocket to be out of.

Well, in the end, when the Boston run was finished, I was given a check for $200 and told to get off somewhere and rewrite the play. I squandered half of this subsidy on the first of four operations performed on a cataracted left eye, and the other half took me to Key West for the rewrite. It was a long rewrite. In fact, it is still going on, though the two hundred bucks are long gone.

Why have I stuck so stubbornly to this play? For seventeen years, in fact? Well, nothing is more precious to anybody than the emotional record of his youth, and you will find the trail of my sleeve-worn heart in this completed play that I now call *Orpheus Descending.* On its surface it was and still is the tale of a wild-spirited boy who wanders into a conventional community of the South and creates the commotion of a fox in a chicken coop.

But beneath that now familiar surface it is a play about unanswered questions that haunt the hearts of people and the difference between continuing to ask them, a difference represented by the four major protagonists of the play, and the acceptance of prescribed answers that are not answers at all, but expedient adaptations or surrender to a state of quandary.

Battle was actually my fifth long play, but the first to be given a professional production. Two of the others, *Candles to the Sun* and *Fugitive Kind,* were produced by a brilliant, but semiprofessional group called The Mummers of St. Louis. A third one, called *Spring Storm,* was written for the late Prof. E. C. Mabie's seminar in playwriting at the University of Iowa, and I read it aloud, appropriately in the spring.

When I had finished reading, the good professor's eyes had a glassy look as though he had drifted into a state of trance. There was a long and all but unendurable silence. Everyone seemed more or less embarrassed. At last the professor pushed back his chair, thus dismissing the seminar, and remarked casually and kindly, "Well, we all have to paint our nudes!" And this is the only reference that I can remember anyone making to the play. That is, in the playwriting class, but I do remember that the late Lemuel Ayers, who was a graduate student at Iowa that year, read it and gave me sufficient praise for its dialogue and atmosphere to reverse my decision to give up the theatre in favor of my other occupation of waiting on tables, or more precisely, handing out trays in the cafeteria of the State Hospital.

Then there was Chicago for a while and a desperate effort to get on the W. P. A. Writers' Project, which didn't succeed, for my work lacked "social content" or "protest" and I couldn't prove that my family was destitute and I still had, in those days, a touch of refinement in my social behavior which made me seem frivolous and decadent to the conscientiously rough-hewn pillars of the Chicago Project.

And so I drifted back to St. Louis, again, and wrote my fourth long play which was the best of the lot. It was called *Not About Nightingales* and it concerned prison life, and I have never written anything since then that could compete with it in violence and horror, for it was based on something that actually occurred along about that time, the literal roasting-alive of a group of intransigent convicts sent for correction to a hot room called "The Klondike."

I submitted it to The Mummers of St. Louis and they were

eager to perform it but they had come to the end of their economic tether and had to disband at this point.

Then there was New Orleans and another effort, while waiting on tables in a restaurant where meals cost only two-bits, to get on a Writers' Project or the Theatre Project, again unsuccessful.

And then there was a wild and wonderful trip to California with a young clarinet player. We ran out of gas in El Paso, also out of cash, and it seemed for days that we would never go farther, but my grandmother was an "easy touch" and I got a letter with a $10 bill stitched neatly to one of the pages, and we continued westward.

In the Los Angeles area, in the summer of 1939, I worked for a while at Clark's Bootery in Culver City, within sight of the M-G-M studio and I lived on a pigeon ranch, and I rode between the two, a distance of ten miles, on a secondhand bicycle that I bought for $5.

Then a most wonderful thing happened. While in New Orleans I had heard about a play contest being conducted by the Group Theatre of New York. I submitted all four of the long plays I have mentioned that preceded *Battle of Angels,* plus a group of one-acts called *American Blues.* One fine day I received, when I returned to the ranch on my bike, a telegram saying that I had won a special award of $100 for the one-acts, and it was signed by Harold Clurman, Molly Day Thacher, who is the present Mrs. Elia Kazan, and that fine writer, Irwin Shaw, the judges of the contest.

I retired from Clark's Bootery and from picking squabs at the pigeon ranch. And the clarinet player and I hopped on our bicycles and rode all the way down to Tiajuana and back as far as Laguna Beach, where we obtained, rent free, a small cabin on a small ranch in return for taking care of the poultry.

We lived all that summer on the $100 from the Group

Theatre and I think it was the happiest summer of my life. All the days were pure gold, the nights were starry, and I looked so young, or carefree, that they would sometimes refuse to sell me a drink because I did not appear to have reached 21. But toward the end of the summer, maybe only because it was the end of the summer as well as the end of the $100, the clarinet player became very moody and disappeared without warning into the San Bernardino Mountains to commune with his soul in solitude, and there was nothing left in the cabin in the canyon but a bag of dried peas.

I lived on stolen eggs and avocados and dried peas for a week, and also on a faint hope stirred by a letter from a lady in New York whose name was Audrey Wood, who had taken hold of all those plays that I had submitted to the Group Theatre contest, and told me that it might be possible to get me one of the Rockefeller Fellowships, or grants, of $1,000 which were being passed out to gifted young writers at that time. And I began to write *Battle of Angels,* a lyrical play about memories and the loneliness of them. Although my beloved grandmother was living on the pension of a retired minister (I believe it was only $85 a month in those days), and her meager earnings as a piano instructor, she once again stitched some bills to a page of a letter, and I took a bus to St. Louis. *Battle of Angels* was finished late that fall and sent to Miss Wood.

One day the phone rang and, in a terrified tone, my mother told me that it was long distance, for me. The voice was Audrey Wood's. Mother waited, shakily, in the doorway. When I hung up I said, quietly, "Rockefeller has given me a $1,000 grant and they want me to come to New York." For the first time since I had known her, my mother burst into tears. "I am so happy," she said. It was all she could say.

And so you see it is a very old play that *Orpheus Descending* has come out of, but a play is never an old one until you quit working on it and I have never quit working on this one, not even now. It never went into the trunk, it always stayed on the work bench, and I am not presenting it now because I have run out of ideas or material for completely new work. I am offering it this season because I honestly believe that it is finally finished. About 75 per cent of it is new writing, but what is much more important, I believe that I have now finally managed to say in it what I wanted to say, and I feel that it now has in it a sort of emotional bridge between those early years described in this article and my present state of existence as a playwright.

So much for the past and present. The future is called "perhaps," which is the only possible thing to call the future. And the important thing is not to allow that to scare you.

Tennessee Williams

ORPHEUS DESCENDING

Orpheus Descending was presented at the Martin Beck Theatre in New York on March 21, 1957, by the Producers Theatre. It was directed by Harold Clurman; the stage set was designed by Boris Aronson, the costumes by Lucinda Ballard, and the lighting by Feder. The cast was as follows:

DOLLY HAMMA	ELIZABETH EUSTIS
BEULAH BINNINGS	JANE ROSE
PEE WEE BINNINGS	WARREN KEMMERLING
DOG HAMMA	DAVID CLARKE
CAROL CUTRERE	LOIS SMITH
EVA TEMPLE	NELL HARRISON
SISTER TEMPLE	MARY FARRELL
UNCLE PLEASANT	JOHN MARRIOTT
VAL XAVIER	CLIFF ROBERTSON
VEE TALBOT	JOANNA ROOS
LADY TORRANCE	MAUREEN STAPLETON
JABE TORRANCE	CRAHAN DENTON
SHERIFF TALBOTT	R. G. ARMSTRONG
MR. DUBINSKY	BEAU TILDEN
WOMAN	JANICE MARS
DAVID CUTRERE	ROBERT WEBBER
NURSE PORTER	VIRGILIA CHEW
FIRST MAN	ALBERT HENDERSON
SECOND MAN	CHARLES TYNER

ACT ONE

SCENE: *The set represents in nonrealistic fashion a general drygoods store and part of a connecting "confectionery" in a small Southern town. The ceiling is high and the upper walls are dark, as if streaked with moisture and cobwebbed. A great dusty window upstage offers a view of disturbing emptiness that fades into late dusk. The action of the play occurs during a rainy season, late winter and early spring, and sometimes the window turns opaque but glistening silver with sheets of rain. "TORRANCE MERCANTILE STORE" is lettered on the window in gilt of old-fashioned design.*

Merchandise is represented very sparsely and it is not realistic. Bolts of pepperel and percale stand upright on large spools, the black skeleton of a dressmaker's dummy stands meaninglessly against a thin white column, and there is a motionless ceiling fan with strips of flypaper hanging from it.

There are stairs that lead to a landing and disappear above it, and on the landing there is a sinister-looking artificial palm tree in a greenish-brown jardiniere.

But the confectionery, which is seen partly through a wide arched door, is shadowy and poetic as some inner dimension of the play.

Another, much smaller, playing area is a tiny bedroom alcove which is usually masked by an Oriental drapery which is worn dim but bears the formal design of a gold tree with scarlet fruit and fantastic birds.

At the rise of the curtain two youngish middle-aged women, DOLLY *and* BEULAH, *are laying out a buffet supper on a pair of pink-and-gray-veined marble-topped tables with gracefully curved black-iron legs, brought into the main area from the confectionery. They are wives of small planters and tastelessly overdressed in a somewhat bizarre fashion.*

3

A train whistles in the distance and dogs bark in response from various points and distances. The women pause in their occupations at the tables and rush to the archway, crying out harshly.

DOLLY: Pee Wee!

BEULAH: Dawg!

DOLLY: Cannonball is comin' into th' depot!

BEULAH: You all git down to th' depot an' meet that train!

[*Their husbands slouch through, heavy, red-faced men in clothes that are too tight for them or too loose, and mud-stained boots.*]

PEE WEE: I fed that one-armed bandit a hunnerd nickels an' it coughed up five.

DOG: Must have hed indigestion.

PEE WEE: I'm gonna speak to Jabe about them slots. [*They go out and a motor starts and pauses.*]

DOLLY: I guess Jabe Torrance has got more to worry about than the slot machines and pinball games in that confectionery.

BEULAH: You're not tellin' a lie. I wint to see Dr. Johnny about Dawg's condition. Dawg's got sugar in his urine again, an as I was leavin' I ast him what was the facks about Jabe Torrance's operation in Mimphis. Well—

DOLLY: What'd he tell you, Beulah?

BEULAH: He said the worse thing a doctor ever can say.

DOLLY: What's that, Beulah?

BEULAH: Nothin' a-tall, not a spoken word did he utter! He just looked at me with those big dark eyes of his and shook his haid like this!

4

DOLLY [*with doleful satisfaction*]: I guess he signed Jabe Torrance's death warrant with just that single silent motion of his haid.

BEULAH: That's exactly what passed through my mind. I understand that they cut him open—[*Pauses to taste something on the table.*]

DOLLY:—An' sewed him right back up!—that's what I heard . . .

BEULAH: I didn't know these olives had seeds in them!

DOLLY: You thought they was stuffed?

BEULAH: Uh-huh. Where's the Temple sisters?

DOLLY: Where d'you think?

BEULAH: Snoopin' aroun' upstairs. If Lady catches 'em at it she'll give those two old maids a touch of her tongue! She's not a Dago for nothin'!

DOLLY: Ha, ha, no! You spoke a true word, honey . . . [*Looks out door as car passes*] Well, I was surprised when I wint up myself!

BEULAH: You wint up you'self?

DOLLY: I did and so did you because I seen you, Beulah.

BEULAH: I never said that I didn't. Curiosity is a human instinct.

DOLLY: They got two separate bedrooms which are not even connectin'. At opposite ends of the hall, and everything is so dingy an' dark up there. Y'know what it seemed like to me? A county jail! I swear to goodness it didn't seem to me like a place for white people to live in!—that's the truth . . .

BEULAH [*darkly*]: Well, I wasn't surprised. Jabe Torrance bought that woman.

5

DOLLY: Bought her?

BEULAH: Yais, he bought her, when she was a girl of eighteen! He bought her and bought her cheap because she'd been thrown over and her heart was broken by that—[*Jerks head toward a passing car, then continues:*]—that Cutrere boy. . . . *Oh,* what a—*Mmmm,* what a—*beautiful* thing he was. . . . And those two met like you struck two stones together and made a fire!—yes—fire . . .

DOLLY: What?

BEULAH: *Fire!*—Ha . . . [*Strikes another match and lights one of the candelabra. Mandolin begins to fade in. The following monologue should be treated frankly as exposition, spoken to audience, almost directly, with a force that commands attention.* DOLLY *does not remain in the playing area, and after the first few sentences, there is no longer any pretense of a duologue.*]

—Well, that was a long time ago, before you and Dog moved into Two River County. Although you must have heard of it. Lady's father was a Wop from the old country and when he first come here with a mandolin and a monkey that wore a little green velvet suit, ha ha.

—He picked up dimes and quarters in the saloons—this was before Prohibition. . . .

—People just called him The Wop, nobody knew his name, just called him 'The Wop,' ha ha ha. . . .

DOLLY [*Off, vaguely*]: Anh-hannnh. . . .

[BEULAH *switches in the chair and fixes the audience with her eyes, leaning slightly forward to compel their attention. Her voice is rich with nostalgia, and at a sign of restlessness, she rises and comes straight out to the proscenium, like a pitchman. This monologue should set the nonrealistic key for the whole production.*]

6

BEULAH: Oh, my law, well, that was Lady's daddy! Then come prohibition an' first thing ennyone knew, The Wop had took to bootleggin' like a duck to water! He picked up a piece of land cheap, it was on the no'th shore of Moon Lake which used to be the old channel of the river and people thought some day the river might swing back that way, and so he got it cheap. . . . [*Moves her chair up closer to proscenium.*] He planted an orchard on it; he covered the whole no'th shore of the lake with grapevines and fruit trees, and then he built little arbors, little white wooden arbors with tables and benches to drink in and carry on in, ha ha! And in the spring and the summer, young couples would come out there, like me and Pee Wee, we used to go out there, an' court up a storm, ha ha, just court up a—storm! Ha ha!— The county was dry in those days, I don't mean dry like now, why, now you just walk a couple of feet off the highway and whistle three times like a jaybird and a nigger pops out of a bush with a bottle of corn!

DOLLY: Ain't that the truth? Ha ha.

BEULAH: But in those days the county was dry for true, I mean bone dry except for The Wop's wine garden. So we'd go out to The Wop's an' drink that Dago red wine an' cut up an' carry on an' raise such cane in those arbors! Why, I remember one Sunday old Doctor Tooker, Methodist minister then, he bust a blood vessel denouncing The Wop in the pulpit!

DOLLY: Lawd have mercy!

BEULAH: Yes, ma'am!—Each of those white wooden arbors had a lamp in it, and one by one, here and there, the lamps would go out as the couples begun to make love . . .

DOLLY: *Oh*—oh . . .

BEULAH: What strange noises you could hear if you listened, calls, cries, whispers, moans—giggles. . . . [*Her voice*

7

is soft with recollection]—And then, one by one, the lamps would be lighted again, and The Wop and his daughter would sing and play Dago songs. . . . [*Bring up mandolin: voice under 'Dicitencello Vuoi.'*] But sometimes The Wop would look around for his daughter, and all of a sudden Lady wouldn't be there!

DOLLY: Where would she be?

BEULAH: She'd be with David Cutrere.

DOLLY: Awwwwww—ha ha . . .

BEULAH:—Carol Cutrere's big brother, Lady and him would disappear in the orchard and old Papa Romano, The Wop, would holler, "Lady, Lady!"—no answer whatsoever, no matter how long he called and no matter how loud. . . .

DOLLY: Well, I guess it's hard to shout back, "Here I am, Papa," when where you are is in the arms of your lover!

BEULAH: Well, that spring, no, it was late that summer . . . [DOLLY *retires again from the playing area.*]—Papa Romano made a bad mistake. He sold liquor to niggers. The Mystic Crew took action. —They rode out there, one night, with gallons of coal oil—it was a real dry summer—and set that place on fire!—They burned the whole thing up, vines, arbors, fruit trees.—Pee Wee and me, we stood on the dance pavilion across the lake and watched that fire spring up. Inside of tin minutes the whole nawth shore of the lake was a mass of flames, a regular sea of flames, and all the way over the lake we could hear Lady's papa shouting, "Fire, fire, fire!"—as if it was necessary to let people know, and the whole sky lit up with it, as red as Guinea red wine! —Ha ha ha ha. . . . Not a fire engine, not a single engine pulled out of a station that night in Two River County!—The poor old fellow, The Wop, he took a blanket and run up into the orchard to fight the fire singlehanded—*and* burned *alive.* . . . Uh-huh! *burned alive.* . . .

8

[*Mandolin stops short.* DOLLY *has returned to the table to have her coffee.*]

You know what I sometimes wonder?

DOLLY: No. What do you wonder?

BEULAH: I wonder sometimes if Lady has any suspicion that her husband, Jabe Torrance, was the leader of the Mystic Crew the night they burned up her father in his wine garden on Moon Lake?

DOLLY: Beulah Binnings, you make my blood run cold with such a thought! How could she live in marriage twenty years with a man if she knew he'd burned her father up in his wine garden?

[*Dog bays in distance.*]

BEULAH: She could live with him in hate. People can live together in hate for a long time, Dolly. Notice their passion for money. I've always noticed when couples don't love each other they develop a passion for money. Haven't you seen that happen? Of course you have. Now there's not many couples that stay devoted forever. Why, some git so they just barely tolerate each other's existence. Isn't that true?

DOLLY: You couldn't of spoken a truer word if you read it out loud from the Bible!

BEULAH: Barely tolerate each other's existence, and some don't even do that. You know, Dolly Hamma, I don't think half as many married min have committed suicide in this county as the Coroner says has done so!

DOLLY: [*with voluptuous appreciation of* BEULAH's *wit*]: You think it's their wives that give them the deep six, honey?

BEULAH: I don't think so, I know so. Why there's couples that loathe and despise the sight, smell and sound of each other before that round-trip honeymoon ticket is punched at both ends, Dolly.

9

DOLLY: I hate to admit it but I can't deny it.

BEULAH: But they hang on together.

DOLLY: Yes, they hang on together.

BEULAH: Year after year after year, accumulating property and money, building up wealth and respect and position in the towns they live in and the counties and cities and the churches they go to, belonging to the clubs and so on and so forth and not a soul but them knowin' they have to go wash their hands after touching something the other one just put down! ha ha ha ha ha!—

DOLLY: Beulah, that's an evil laugh of yours, that laugh of yours is evil!

BEULAH [*louder*]: Ha ha ha ha ha!—But you know it's the truth.

DOLLY: Yes, she's tellin' the truth! [*Nods to audience.*]

BEULAH: Then one of them—gits—*cincer* or has a—*stroke* or somethin'?—The other one—

DOLLY:—Hauls in the loot?

BEULAH: That's right, hauls in the loot! Oh, my, then you should see how him or her blossoms out. New house, new car, new clothes. Some of 'em even change to a different church!—If it's a widow, she goes with a younger man, and if it's a widower, he starts courtin' some chick, ha ha ha ha ha!

And so I said, I said to Lady this morning before she left for Mamphis to bring Jabe home, I said, "Lady, I don't suppose you're going to reopen the confectionery till Jabe is completely recovered from his operation." She said, "It can't wait for anything that might take that much time." Those are her exact words. It can't wait for anything that might take that much time. Too much is invested in it. It's going to be done over, redecorated, and opened on schedule the Saturday

10

before Easter this spring!—Why?—Because—she knows Jabe is dying and she wants to clean up quick!

DOLLY: An awful thought. But a true one. Most awful thoughts are.

[*They are startled by sudden light laughter from the dim upstage area. The light changes on the stage to mark a division.*]

SCENE ONE

The women turn to see CAROL CUTRERE *in the archway
between the store and the confectionery. She is past thirty and,
lacking prettiness, she has an odd, fugitive beauty which is
stressed, almost to the point of fantasy, by a style of makeup
with which a dancer named Valli has lately made such an impression in the bohemian centers of France and Italy, the face
and lips powdered white and the eyes outlined and exaggerated
with black pencil and the lids tinted blue. Her family name is
the oldest and most distinguished in the country.*

BEULAH: Somebody don't seem to know that the store is
closed.

DOLLY: Beulah?

BEULAH: What?

DOLLY: Can you understand how anybody would deliberately make themselves look fantastic as that?

BEULAH: Some people have to show off, it's a passion with
them, anything on earth to get attention.

DOLLY: I sure wouldn't care for that kind of attention. Not
me. I wouldn't desire it. . . .

[*During these lines, just loud enough for her to hear them,*
CAROL *has crossed to the pay-phone and deposited a coin.*]

CAROL: I want Tulane 0370 in New Orleans. What? Oh.
Hold on a minute.

[EVA TEMPLE *is descending the stairs, slowly, as if awed by*
CAROL'S *appearance.* CAROL *rings open the cashbox and
removes some coins; returns to deposit coins in phone.*]

BEULAH: She helped herself to money out of the cashbox.

[EVA *passes* CAROL *like a timid child skirting a lion cage.*]

12

CAROL: Hello, Sister.

EVA: I'm Eva.

CAROL: Hello, Eva.

EVA: Hello . . . [*Then in a loud whisper to* BEULAH *and* DOLLY:] She took money out of the cashbox.

DOLLY: Oh, she can do as she pleases, she's a Cutrere!

BEULAH: Shoot . . .

EVA: What is she doin' barefooted?

BEULAH: The last time she was arrested on the highway, they say that she was naked under her coat.

CAROL [*to operator*]: I'm waiting. [*Then to women:*]—I caught the heel of my slipper in that rotten boardwalk out there and it broke right off. [*Raises slippers in hand.*] They say if you break the heel of your slipper in the morning it means you'll meet the love of your life before dark. But it was already dark when I broke the heel of my slipper. Maybe that means I'll meet the love of my life before daybreak. [*The quality of her voice is curiously clear and childlike.* SISTER TEMPLE *appears on stair landing bearing an old waffle iron.*]

SISTER: Wasn't that them?

EVA: No, it was Carol Cutrere!

CAROL [*at phone*]: Just keep on ringing, please, he's probably drunk.

[SISTER *crosses by her as* EVA *did.*]

Sometimes it takes quite a while to get through the living-room furniture. . . .

SISTER:—She a *sight?*

EVA: Uh-huh!

CAROL: Bertie?—Carol!—Hi, doll! Did you trip over something? I heard a crash. Well, I'm leaving right now, I'm already on the highway and everything's fixed, I've got my allowance back on condition that I remain forever away from Two River County! I had to blackmail them a little. I came to dinner with my eyes made up and my little black sequin jacket and Betsy Boo, my brother's wife, said, "Carol, you going out to a fancy dress ball?" I said, "Oh, no, I'm just going jooking tonight up and down the Dixie Highway between here and Memphis like I used to when I lived here." Why, honey, she flew so fast you couldn't see her passing and came back in with the ink still wet on the check! And this will be done once a month as long as I stay away from Two River County. . . . [*Laughs gaily.*]—How's Jackie? Bless his heart, give him a sweet kiss for me! Oh, honey, I'm driving straight through, not even stopping for pickups unless you need one! I'll meet you in the Starlite Lounge before it closes, or if I'm irresistibly delayed, I'll certainly join you for coffee at the Morning Call before the all-night places have closed for the day . . . —I—Bertie? Bertie? [*Laughs uncertainly and hangs up.*]—let's see, now. . . . [*Removes a revolver from her trench-coat pocket and crosses to fill it with cartridges back of counter.*]

EVA: What she looking for?

SISTER: Ask her.

EVA [*advancing*]: What're you looking for, Carol?

CAROL: Cartridges for my revolver.

DOLLY: She don't have a license to carry a pistol.

BEULAH: She don't have a license to drive a car.

CAROL: When I stop for someone I want to be sure it's someone I want to stop for.

DOLLY: Sheriff Talbott ought to know about this when he gits back from the depot.

CAROL: Tell him, ladies. I've already given him notice that if he ever attempts to stop me again on the highway, I'll shoot it out with him. . . .

BEULAH: When anybody has trouble with the law—

[*Her sentence is interrupted by a panicky scream from* EVA, *immediately repeated by* SISTER. *The* TEMPLE SISTERS *scramble upstairs to the landing.* DOLLY *also cries out and turns, covering her face. A Negro* CONJURE MAN *has entered the store. His tattered garments are fantastically bedizened with many talismans and good-luck charms of shell and bone and feather. His blue-black skin is daubed with cryptic signs in white paint.*]

DOLLY: Git him out, git him out, he's going to mark my baby!

BEULAH: Oh, shoot, Dolly. . . .

[DOLLY *has now fled after the* TEMPLE SISTERS, *to the landing of the stairs. The* CONJURE MAN *advances with a soft, rapid, toothless mumble of words that sound like wind in dry grass. He is holding out something in his shaking hand.*]

It's just that old crazy conjure man from Blue Mountain. He cain't mark your baby.

[*Phrase of primitive music or percussion as* NEGRO *moves into light.* BEULAH *follows* DOLLY *to landing.*]

CAROL [*very high and clear voice*]: Come here, Uncle, and let me see what you've got there. Oh, it's a bone of some kind. No, I don't want to touch it, it isn't clean yet, there's still some flesh clinging to it.

15

[*Women make sounds of revulsion.*]

Yes, I know it's the breastbone of a bird but it's still tainted with corruption. Leave it a long time on a bare rock in the rain and the sun till every sign of corruption is burned and washed away from it, and then it will be a good charm, a white charm, but now it's a black charm, Uncle. So take it away and do what I told you with it. . . .

[*The* NEGRO *makes a ducking obeisance and shuffles slowly back to the door.*]

Hey, Uncle Pleasant, give us the Choctaw cry.

[NEGRO *stops in confectionery.*]

He's part Choctaw, he knows the Choctaw cry.

SISTER TEMPLE: Don't let him holler in *here!*

CAROL: Come on, Uncle Pleasant, *you* know it!

[*She takes off her coat and sits on the R. window sill. She starts the cry herself. The* NEGRO *throws back his head and completes it: a series of barking sounds that rise to a high sustained note of wild intensity. The women on the landing retreat further upstairs. Just then, as though the cry had brought him,* VAL *enters the store. He is a young man, about 30, who has a kind of wild beauty about him that the cry would suggest. He does not wear Levi's or a T-shirt, he has on a pair of dark serge pants, glazed from long wear and not excessively tight-fitting. His remarkable garment is a snakeskin jacket, mottled white, black and gray. He carries a guitar which is covered with inscriptions.*]

CAROL [*looking at the young man*]: Thanks, Uncle . . .

BEULAH: *Hey, old man, you! Choctaw! Conjure man! Nigguh! Will you go out-a this sto'? So we can come back down stairs?*

[CAROL *hands* NEGRO *a dollar; he goes out right cackling.*

16

VAL *holds the door open for* VEE TALBOTT, *a heavy, vague woman in her forties. She does primitive oil paintings and carries one into the store, saying:*]

VEE: I got m'skirt caught in th' door of the Chevrolet an' I'm afraid I tore it.

[*The women descend into store: laconic greetings, interest focused on* VAL.]

Is it dark in here or am I losin' my eyesight? I been painting all day, finished a picture in a ten-hour stretch, just stopped a few minutes fo' coffee and went back to it again while I had a clear vision. I think I got it this time. But I'm so exhausted I could drop in my tracks. There's nothing more exhausting than that kind of work on earth, it's not so much that it tires your body out, but it leaves you drained inside. Y'know what I mean? Inside? Like you was burned out by something? Well! Still! —You feel you've accomplished something when you're through with it, sometimes you feel—*elevated!* How are you, Dolly?

DOLLY: All right, Mrs. Talbott.

VEE: That's good. How are *you*, Beulah?

BEULAH: Oh, I'm all right, I reckon.

VEE: Still can't make out much. Who is that there? [*Indicates* CAROL'S *figure by the window. A significant silence greets this question.* VEE, *suddenly:*]

Oh! I thought her folks had got her out of the county . . .

[CAROL *utters a very light, slightly rueful laugh, her eyes drifting back to* VAL *as she moves back into confectionery.*]

Jabe and Lady back yet?

DOLLY: Pee Wee an' Dawg have gone to the depot to meet 'em.

17

VEE: Aw. Well, I'm just in time. I brought my new picture with me, the paint isn't dry on it yet. I thought that Lady might want to hang it up in Jabe's room while he's con-valescin' from the operation, cause after a close shave with death, people like to be reminded of spiritual things. Huh? Yes! This is the Holy Ghost ascending. . . .

DOLLY [*looking at canvas*]: You didn't put a head on it.

VEE: The head was a blaze of light, that's all I saw in my vision.

DOLLY: Who's the young man with yuh?

VEE: Aw, excuse me, I'm too worn out to have manners. This is Mr. Valentine Xavier, Mrs. Hamma and Mrs.—I'm sorry, Beulah. I never *can* get y' last *name!*

BEULAH: I fo'give you. My name is Beulah Binnings.

VAL: What shall I do with this here?

VEE: Oh, that bowl of sherbet. I thought that Jabe might need something light an' digestible so I brought a bowl of sherbet.

DOLLY: What flavor is it?

VEE: Pineapple.

DOLLY: Oh, goody, I love pineapple. Better put it in the icebox before it starts to melt.

BEULAH [*looking under napkin that covers bowl*]: I'm afraid you're lockin' th' stable after the horse is gone.

DOLLY: Aw, is it melted already?

BEULAH: Reduced to juice.

VEE: Aw, shoot. Well, put it on ice anyhow, it might thicken up.

[*Women are still watching* VAL.]

18

Where's the icebox?

BEULAH: In the confectionery.

VEE: I thought that Lady had closed the confectionery.

BEULAH: Yes, but the Frigidaire's still there.

[VAL *goes out R. through confectionery.*]

VEE: Mr. Xavier is a stranger in our midst. His car broke down in that storm last night and I let him sleep in the lockup. He's lookin' for work and I thought I'd introduce him to Lady an' Jabe because if Jabe can't work they're going to need somebody to help out in th' store.

BEULAH: That's a good idea.

DOLLY: Uh-huh.

BEULAH: Well, come on in, you all, it don't look like they're comin' straight home from the depot anyhow.

DOLLY: Maybe that wasn't the Cannonball Express.

BEULAH: Or maybe they stopped off fo' Pee Wee to buy some liquor.

DOLLY: Yeah . . . at Ruby Lightfoot's.

[*They move past* CAROL *and out of sight.* CAROL *has risen. Now she crosses into the main store area, watching* VAL *with the candid curiosity of one child observing another. He pays no attention but concentrates on his belt buckle which he is repairing with a pocketknife.*]

CAROL: What're you fixing?

VAL: Belt buckle.

CAROL: Boys like you are always fixing something. Could you fix my slipper?

VAL: What's wrong with your slipper?

19

CAROL: Why are you pretending not to remember me?

VAL: It's hard to remember someone you never met.

CAROL: Then why'd you look so startled when you saw me?

VAL: Did I?

CAROL: I thought for a moment you'd run back out the door.

VAL: The sight of a woman can make me walk in a hurry but I don't think it's ever made me run.—You're standing in my light.

CAROL [*moving aside slightly*]: Oh, excuse me. Better?

VAL: Thanks. . . .

CAROL: Are you afraid I'll snitch?

VAL: Do what?

CAROL: Snitch? I wouldn't; I'm not a snitch. But I can prove that I know you if I have to. It was New Year's Eve in New Orleans.

VAL: I need a small pair of pliers. . . .

CAROL: You had on that jacket and a snake ring with a ruby eye.

VAL: I never had a snake ring with a ruby eye.

CAROL: A snake ring with an emerald eye?

VAL: I never had a snake ring with any kind of an eye. . . . [*Begins to whistle softly, his face averted.*]

CAROL [*smiling gently*]: Then maybe it was a dragon ring with an emerald eye or a diamond or a ruby eye. You told us that it was a gift from a lady osteopath that you'd met somewhere in your travels and that any time you were broke you'd wire this lady osteopath collect, and no matter how far you were or how long it was since you'd seen her, she'd send

20

you a money order for twenty-five dollars with the same sweet message each time. "I love you. When will you come back?" And to prove the story, not that it was difficult to believe it, you took the latest of these sweet messages from your wallet for us to see. . . . [*She throws back her head with soft laughter. He looks away still further and busies himself with the belt buckle.*]—We followed you through five places before we made contact with you and I was the one that made contact. I went up to the bar where you were standing and touched your jacket and said, "What stuff is this made of?" and when you said it was snakeskin, I said, "I wish you'd told me before I touched it." And you said something not nice. You said, "Maybe that will learn you to hold back your hands." I was drunk by that time which was after midnight. Do you remember what I said to you? I said, "What on earth can you do on this earth but catch at whatever comes near you, with both your hands, until your fingers are broken?" I'd never said that before, or even consciously thought it, but afterwards it seemed like the truest thing that my lips had ever spoken, what on earth can you do but catch at whatever comes near you with both your hands until your fingers are broken. . . . You gave me a quick, sober look. I think you nodded slightly, and then you picked up your guitar and began to sing. After singing you passed the kitty. Whenever paper money was dropped in the kitty you blew a whistle. My cousin Bertie and I dropped in five dollars, you blew the whistle five times and then sat down at our table for a drink, Schenley's with Seven Up. You showed us all those signatures on your guitar. . . . Any correction so far?

VAL: Why are you so anxious to prove I know you?

CAROL: Because I want to know you better and better! I'd like to go out jooking with you tonight.

VAL: What's jooking?

CAROL: Oh, don't you know what that is? That's where you get in a car and drink a little and drive a little and stop and dance a little to a juke box and then you drink a little more and drive a little more and stop and dance a little more to a juke box and then you stop dancing and you just drink and drive and then you stop driving and just drink, and then, finally, you stop drinking. . . .

VAL:—What do you do, then?

CAROL: That depends on the weather and who you're jooking with. If it's a clear night you spread a blanket among the memorial stones on Cypress Hill, which is the local bone orchard, but if it's not a fair night, and this one certainly isn't, why, usually then you go to the Idlewild cabins between here and Sunset on the Dixie Highway. . . .

VAL:—That's about what I figured. But I don't go that route. Heavy drinking and smoking the weed and shacking with strangers is okay for kids in their twenties but this is my thirtieth birthday and I'm all through with that route. [*Looks up with dark eyes.*] I'm not young any more.

CAROL: You're young at thirty—I hope so! I'm twenty-nine!

VAL: Naw, you're not young at thirty if you've been on a Goddam party since you were fifteen!

[*Picks up his guitar and sings and plays "Heavenly Grass."* CAROL *has taken a pint of bourbon from her trench-coat pocket and she passes it to him.*]

CAROL: Thanks. That's lovely. Many happy returns of your birthday, Snakeskin.

[*She is very close to him.* VEE *enters and says sharply:*]

VEE: Mr. Xavier don't drink.

CAROL: Oh, ex-cuse *me!*

VEE: And if you behaved yourself better your father would not be paralyzed in bed!

[*Sound of car out front. Women come running with various cries.* LADY *enters, nodding to the women, and holding the door open for her husband and the men following him. She greets the women in almost toneless murmurs, as if too tired to speak. She could be any age between thirty-five and forty-five, in appearance, but her figure is youthful. Her face taut. She is a woman who met with emotional disaster in her girlhood; verges on hysteria under strain. Her voice is often shrill and her body tense. But when in repose, a girlish softness emerges again and she looks ten years younger.*]

LADY: Come in, Jabe. We've got a reception committee here to meet us. They've set up a buffet supper.

[JABE *enters. A gaunt, wolfish man, gray and yellow. The women chatter idiotically.*]

BEULAH: Well, look who's here!

DOLLY: Well, *Jabe!*

BEULAH: I don't think he's been sick. I think he's been to Miami. Look at that wonderful color in his face!

DOLLY: I never seen him look better in my life!

BEULAH: Who does he think he's foolin'? Ha ha ha!— not *me!*

JABE: Whew, Jesus—I'm mighty—tired. . . .

[*An uncomfortable silence, everyone staring greedily at the dying man with his tense, wolfish smile and nervous cough.*]

PEE WEE: Well, Jabe, we been feedin' lots of nickels to those one-arm bandits in there.

DOG: An' that pinball machine is hotter'n a pistol.

PEE WEE: Ha ha.

23

[EVA TEMPLE *appears on stairs and screams for her sister.*]

EVA: Sistuh! Sistuh! Sistuh! Cousin Jabe's here!

[*A loud clatter upstairs and shrieks.*]

JABE: Jesus. . . .

[EVA *rushing at him—stops short and bursts into tears.*]

LADY: Oh, cut that out, Eva Temple!—What were you doin' upstairs? ·

EVA: I can't help it, it's so good to see him, it's so wonderful to see our cousin again, oh, Jabe, *blessed!*

SISTER: Where's Jabe, where's precious Jabe? Where's our precious cousin?

EVA: Right here, Sister!

SISTER: Well, bless your old sweet life, and lookit the color he's got in his face, will you?

BEULAH: I just told him he looks like he's been to Miami and got a Florida suntan, haha ha!

[*The preceding speeches are very rapid, all overlapping.*]

JABE: I ain't been out in no sun an' if you all will excuse me I'm gonna do my celebratin' upstairs in bed because I'm kind of—worn out. [*Goes creakily to foot of steps while* EVA *and* SISTER *sob into their handkerchiefs behind him.*]—I see they's been some changes made here. Uh-huh. Uh-huh. How come the shoe department's back here now? [*Instant hostility as if habitual between them.*]

LADY: We always had a problem with light in this store.

JABE: So you put the shoe department further away from the window? That's sensible. A very intelligent solution to the problem, Lady.

24

LADY: Jabe, you know I told you we got a fluorescent tube coming to put back here.

JABE: Uh-huh. Uh-huh. Well. Tomorrow I'll get me some niggers to help me move the shoe department back front.

LADY: You do whatever you want to, it's your store.

JABE: Uh-huh. Uh-huh. I'm glad you reminded me of it.

[LADY *turns sharply away. He starts up stairs.* PEE WEE *and* DOG *follow him up. The women huddle and whisper in the store.* LADY *sinks wearily into chair at table.*]

BEULAH: That man will never come down those stairs again!

DOLLY: Never in this world, honey.

BEULAH: He has th' death sweat on him! Did you notice that death sweat on him?

DOLLY: An' yellow as butter, just as yellow as—

[SISTER *sobs.*]

EVA: Sister, Sister!

BEULAH [*crossing to* LADY]: Lady, I don't suppose you feel much like talking about it right now but Dog and me are so worried.

DOLLY: Pee Wee and me are worried sick about it.

LADY:—About what?

BEULAH: Jabe's operation in Memphis. Was it successful?

DOLLY: Wasn't it successful?

[LADY *stares at them blindly. The women, except* CAROL, *close avidly about her, tense with morbid interest.*]

SISTER: Was it too late for surgical interference?

EVA: Wasn't it successful?

[*A loud, measured knock begins on the floor above.*]

BEULAH: Somebody told us it had gone past the knife.

DOLLY: We do hope it ain't hopeless.

EVA: We hope and pray it ain't hopeless.

[*All their faces wear faint, unconscious smiles.* LADY *looks from face to face; then utters a slight, startled laugh and springs up from the table and crosses to the stairs.*]

LADY [*as if in flight*]: Excuse me, I have to go up, Jabe's knocking for me. [LADY *goes upstairs. The women gaze after her.*]

CAROL [*suddenly and clearly, in the silence*]: Speaking of knocks, I have a knock in my engine. It goes knock, knock, and I say who's there. I don't know whether I'm in communication with some dead ancestor or the motor's about to drop out and leave me stranded in the dead of night on the Dixie Highway. Do you have any knowledge of mechanics? I'm sure you do. Would you be sweet and take a short drive with me? So you could hear that knock?

VAL: I don't have time.

CAROL: What have you got to do?

VAL: I'm waiting to see about a job in this store.

CAROL: I'm offering you a job.

VAL: I want a job that pays.

CAROL: I expect to pay you.

[*Women whisper loudly in the background.*]

VAL: Maybe sometime tomorrow.

CAROL: I can't stay here overnight; I'm not allowed to stay overnight in this county.

[*Whispers rise. The word "corrupt" is distinguished.*]

26

[*Without turning, smiling very brightly:*] What are they saying about me? Can you hear what those women are saying about me?

VAL:—Play it cool. . . .

CAROL: I don't like playing it cool! What are they saying about me? That I'm corrupt?

VAL: If you don't want to be talked about, why do you make up like that, why do you—

CAROL: *To show off!*

VAL: What?

CAROL: *I'm an exhibitionist!* I want to be noticed, seen, heard, felt! I want them to know I'm alive! Don't you want them to know you're alive?

VAL: I want to live and I don't care if they know I'm alive or not.

CAROL: Then why do you play a guitar?

VAL: Why do you make a Goddam show of yourself?

CAROL: That's right, for the same reason.

VAL: We don't go the same route. . . . [*He keeps moving away from her; she continually follows him. Her speech is compulsive.*]

CAROL: I used to be what they call a Christ-bitten reformer. You know what that is?—A kind of benign exhibitionist. . . . I delivered stump speeches, wrote letters of protest about the gradual massacre of the colored majority in the county. I thought it was wrong for pellagra and slow starvation to cut them down when the cotton crop failed from army worm or boll weevil or too much rain in summer. I wanted to, tried to, put up free clinics, I squandered the money my mother left me on it. And when that Willie McGee thing came along—

27

he was sent to the chair for having improper relations with a white whore—[*Her voice is like a passionate incantation.*] I made a fuss about it. I put on a potato sack and set out for the capitol on foot. This was in winter. I walked barefoot in this burlap sack to deliver a personal protest to the Governor of the State. Oh, I suppose it was partly exhibitionism on my part, but it wasn't completely exhibitionism; there was something else in it, too. You know how far I got? Six miles out of town—hooted, jeered at, even spit on!—every step of the way—and then arrested! Guess what for? Lewd vagrancy! Uh-huh, that was the charge, "lewd vagrancy," because they said that potato sack I had on was not a respectable garment. . . . Well, all that was a pretty long time ago, and now I'm not a reformer any more. I'm just a "lewd vagrant." And I'm showing the "S.O.B.S." how lewd a "lewd vagrant" can be if she puts her whole heart in it like I do mine! All right. I've told you my story, the story of an exhibitionist. Now I want you to do something for me. Take me out to Cypress Hill in my car. And we'll hear the dead people talk. They do talk there. They chatter together like birds on Cypress Hill, but all they say is one word and that one word is "live," they say "Live, live, live, live, live!" It's all they've learned, it's the only advice they can give.—Just live. . . . [*She opens the door.*] Simple!—a very simple instruction. . . .

[*Goes out. Women's voices rise from the steady, indistinct murmur, like hissing geese.*]

WOMEN'S VOICES:—No, not liquor! Dope!

—Something not normal all right!

—Her father and brother were warned by the Vigilantes to keep her out of this county.

—She's absolutely degraded!

—Yes, corrupt!

—Corrupt! (Etc., etc.)

[*As if repelled by their hissing voices,* VAL *suddenly picks up his guitar and goes out of the store as—*VEE TALBOTT *appears on the landing and calls down to him.*]

VEE: Mr. Xavier! Where is Mr. Xavier?

BEULAH: Gone, honey.

DOLLY: You might as well face it, Vee. This is one candidate for salvation that you have lost to the opposition.

BEULAH: He's gone off to Cypress Hill with the Cutrere girl.

VEE [*descending*]:—If some of you older women in Two River County would set a better example there'd be more decent young people!

BEULAH: What was that remark?

VEE: I mean that people who give drinkin' parties an' get so drunk they don't know which is their husband and which is somebody else's and people who serve on the altar guild and still play cards on Sundays—

BEULAH: Just stop right there! Now I've discovered the source of that dirty gossip!

VEE: I'm only repeating what I've been told by others. I never been to these parties!

BEULAH: No, and you never will! You're a public kill-joy, a professional hypocrite!

VEE: I try to build up characters! You and your drinkin' parties are only concerned with tearin' characters down! I'm goin' upstairs, I'm goin' back upstairs! [*Rushes upstairs.*]

BEULAH: Well, I'm glad I said what I said to that woman. I've got no earthly patience with that sort of hypocriticism.

Dolly, let's put this perishable stuff in the Frigidaire and leave here. I've never been so thoroughly disgusted!

DOLLY: Oh, my Lawd. [*Pauses at stairs and shouts:*] PEE WEE! [*Goes off with the dishes.*]

SISTER: Both of those wimmen are as common as dirt.

EVA: Dolly's folks in Blue Mountain are nothin' at all but the poorest kind of white trash. Why, Lollie Tucker told me the old man sits on the porch with his shoes off drinkin' beer out of a bucket!—Let's take these flowers with us to put on the altar.

SISTER: Yes, we can give Jabe credit in the parish notes.

EVA: I'm going to take these olive-nut sandwiches, too. They'll come in handy for the Bishop Adjutant's tea.

[DOLLY *and* BEULAH *cross through.*]

DOLLY: We still have time to make the second show.

BEULAH [*shouting*]: Dog!

DOLLY: Pee Wee! [*They rush out of store.*]

EVA: Sits on the porch with his shoes off?

SISTER: Drinkin' beer out of a bucket! [*They go out with umbrellas, etc. Men descend stairs.*]

SHERIFF TALBOTT: Well, it looks to me like Jabe will more than likely go under before the cotton comes up.

PEE WEE: He never looked good.

DOG: Naw, but now he looks worse.

[*They cross to door.*]

SHERIFF: Vee!

VEE [*from landing*]: Hush that bawling. I had to speak to Lady about that boy and I couldn't speak to her in front of

Jabe because he thinks he's gonna be able to go back to work himself.

SHERIFF: Well, move along, quit foolin'.

VEE: I think I ought to wait till that boy gits back.

SHERIFF: I'm sick of you making a goddam fool of yourself over every stray bastard that wanders into this county.

[*Car horn honks loudly.* VEE *follows her husband out. Sound of cars driving off. Dogs bay in distance as lights dim to indicate short passage of time.*]

A couple of hours later that night. Through the great window the landscape is faintly luminous under a scudding moonlit sky. Outside a girl's laughter, CAROL'S, *rings out high and clear and is followed by the sound of a motor, rapidly going off.*

VAL *enters the store before the car sound quite fades out and while a dog is still barking at it somewhere along the highway. He says "Christ" under his breath, goes to the buffet table and scrubs lipstick stain off his mouth and face with a paper napkin, picks up his guitar which he had left on a counter.*

Footsteps descending: LADY *appears on the landing in a flannel robe, shivering in the cold air; she snaps her fingers impatiently for the old dog, Bella, who comes limping down beside her. She doesn't see* VAL, *seated on the shadowy counter, and she goes directly to the phone near the stairs. Her manner is desperate, her voice harsh and shrill.*

LADY: Ge' me the drugstore, will you? I know the drugstore's closed, this is Mrs. Torrance, my store's closed, too, but I got a sick man here, just back from the hospital, yeah, yeah, an emergency, wake up Mr. Dubinsky, keep ringing till he answers, it's an emergency! [*Pause: she mutters under her breath:*] —Porca la miseria!—I wish I was dead, dead, dead. . . .

VAL [*quietly*]: No, you don't, lady.

[*She gasps, turning and seeing him, without leaving the phone, she rings the cashbox open and snatches out something.*]

LADY: What're you doin' here? You know this store is closed!

VAL: I seen a light was still on and the door was open so I come back to—

LADY: You see what I got in my hand? [*Raises revolver above level of counter.*]

VAL: You going to shoot me?

LADY: You better believe it if you don't get out of here, mister!

VAL: That's all right, Lady, I just come back to pick up my guitar.

LADY: To pick up your guitar?

[*He lifts it gravely.*]

—Huh. . . .

VAL: Miss Talbott brought me here. I was here when you got back from Memphis, don't you remember?

LADY:—Aw. Aw, yeah. . . . You been here all this time?

VAL: No. I went out and come back.

LADY [*into the phone*]: I told you to keep ringing till he answers! Go on, keep ringing, keep ringing! [*Then to* VAL:] You went out and come back?

VAL: Yeah.

LADY: What for?

VAL: You know that girl that was here?

LADY: Carol Cutrere?

VAL: She said she had car trouble and could I fix it.

LADY:—Did you fix it?

VAL: She didn't have no car trouble, that wasn't her trouble, oh, she had trouble, all right, but *that* wasn't it. . . .

LADY: What was her trouble?

VAL: She made a mistake about me.

LADY: What mistake?

VAL: She thought I had a sign "Male at Stud" hung on me.

LADY: She thought you—? [*Into phone suddenly:*] Oh, Mr. Dubinsky, I'm sorry to wake you up but I just brought my husband back from the Memphis hospital and I left my box of luminal tablets in the—I got to have some! I ain't slep' for three nights, I'm going to pieces, you hear me, I'm going to pieces, I ain't slept in three nights, I got to have some tonight. Now you look here, if you want to keep my trade, you send me over some tablets. Then bring them yourself, God damn it, excuse my French! Because I'm going to pieces right this minute! [*Hangs up violently.*]—*Mannage la miseria!*—Christ. . . . I'm shivering!—It's cold as a Goddam ice-plant in this store, I don't know why, it never seems to hold heat, the ceiling's too high or something, it don't hold heat at all.—Now what do you want? I got to go upstairs.

VAL: Here. Put this on you.

[*He removes his jacket and hands it to her. She doesn't take it at once, stares at him questioningly and then slowly takes the jacket in her hands and examines it, running her fingers curiously over the snakeskin.*]

LADY: What is this stuff this thing's made of? It looks like it was snakeskin.

VAL: Yeah, well, that's what it is.

LADY: What're you doing with a snakeskin jacket?

VAL: It's a sort of a trademark; people call me Snakeskin.

LADY: Who calls you Snakeskin?

VAL: Oh, in the bars, the sort of places I work in—but I've quit that. I'm through with that stuff now. . . .

LADY: You're a—entertainer?

VAL: I sing and play the guitar.

LADY:—Aw? [*She puts the jacket on as if to explore it.*] It feels warm all right.

VAL: It's warm from my body, I guess. . . .

LADY: You must be a warm-blooded boy. . . .

VAL: That's right. . . .

LADY: Well, what in God's name are you lookin' for around here?

VAL:—Work.

LADY: Boys like you don't work.

VAL: What d'you mean by boys like me?

LADY: Ones that play th' guitar and go around talkin' about how warm they are. . . .

VAL: That happens t' be the truth. My temperature's always a couple degrees above normal the same as a dog's, it's normal for me the same as it is for a dog, that's the truth. . . .

LADY:—Huh!

VAL: You don't believe me?

LADY: I have no reason to doubt you, but what about it?

VAL:—Why—nothing. . . .

[LADY *laughs softly and suddenly;* VAL *smiles slowly and warmly.*]

LADY: You're a peculiar somebody all right, you sure are! How did you get around here?

VAL: I was driving through here last night and an axle broke on my car, that stopped me here, and I went to the county jail for a place to sleep out of the rain. Mizz Talbott

35

took me in and give me a cot in the lockup and said if I hung
around till you got back that you might give me a job in the
store to help out since your husband was tooken sick.

LADY:—Uh-huh. Well—she was wrong about that. . . .
If I took on help here it would have to be local help, I
couldn't hire no stranger with a—snakeskin jacket and a guitar
. . . and that runs a temperature as high as a dog's! [*Throws
back her head in another soft, sudden laugh and starts to take
off the jacket.*]

VAL: Keep it on.

LADY: No, I got to go up now and you had better be
going . . .

VAL: I got nowhere to go.

LADY: Well, everyone's got a problem and that's yours.

VAL:—What nationality are you?

LADY: Why do you ask me that?

VAL: You seem to be like a foreigner.

LADY: I'm the daughter of a Wop bootlegger burned to
death in his orchard!—Take your jacket. . . .

VAL: What was that you said about your father?

LADY: Why?

VAL:—A "Wop bootlegger"?

LADY:—They burned him to death in his orchard! What
about it? The story's well known around here.

[JABE *knocks on ceiling.*]

I got to go up, I'm being called for.

[*She turns out light over counter and at the same moment
he begins to sing softly with his guitar: "Heavenly Grass."
He suddenly stops short and says abruptly:*]

36

VAL: I do electric repairs.

[LADY *stares at him softly.*]

I can do all kinds of odd jobs. Lady, I'm thirty today and I'm through with the life that I've been leading. [*Pause. Dog bays in distance.*] I lived in corruption but I'm not corrupted. Here is why. [*Picks up his guitar.*] My life's companion! It washes me clean like water when anything unclean has touched me. . . . [*Plays softly, with a slow smile.*]

LADY: What's all that writing on it?

VAL: Autographs of musicians I run into here and there.

LADY: Can I see it?

VAL: Turn on that light above you.

[*She switches on green-shaded bulb over counter.* VAL *holds the instrument tenderly between them as if it were a child; his voice is soft, intimate, tender.*]

See this name? Leadbelly?

LADY: Leadbelly?

VAL: Greatest man ever lived on the twelve-string guitar! Played it so good he broke the stone heart of a Texas governor with it and won himself a pardon out of jail. . . . And see this name Oliver? King Oliver? That name is immortal, Lady. Greatest man since Gabriel on a horn. . . .

LADY: What's this name?

VAL: Oh. That name? That name is also immortal. The name Bessie Smith is written in the stars!—Jim Crow killed her, John Barleycorn and Jim Crow killed Bessie Smith but that's another story. . . . See this name here? That's another immortal!

LADY: Fats Waller? Is his name written in the stars, too?

37

VAL: Yes, his name is written in the stars, too. . . .

[*Her voice is also intimate and soft: a spell of softness between them, their bodies almost touching, only divided by the guitar.*]

LADY: You had any sales experience?

VAL: All my life I been selling something to someone.

LADY: So's everybody. You got any character reference on you?

VAL: I have this—letter.

[*Removes a worn, folded letter from a wallet, dropping a lot of snapshots and cards of various kinds on the floor. He passes the letter to her gravely and crouches to collect the dropped articles while she peruses the character reference.*]

LADY [*reading slowly aloud*]: "This boy worked for me three months in my auto repair shop and is a real hard worker and is good and honest but is a peculiar talker and that is the reason I got to let him go but would like to—[*Holds letter closer to light.*]—would like to—keep him. Yours truly."

[VAL *stares at her gravely, blinking a little.*]

Huh!—Some reference!

VAL:—Is that what it says?

LADY: Didn't you know what it said?

VAL: No.—The man sealed the envelope on it.

LADY: Well, that's not the sort of character reference that will do you much good, boy.

VAL: Naw. I guess it ain't.

LADY:—However. . . .

VAL:—What?

LADY: What people say about you don't mean much. Can you read shoe sizes?

VAL: I guess so.

LADY: What does 75 David mean?

[VAL *stares at her, shakes head slowly.*]

75 means seven and one half long and David mean "D" wide. You know how to make change?

VAL: Yeah, I could make change in a store.

LADY: Change for better or worse? Ha ha!—Well— [*Pause.*] Well—you see that other room there, through that arch there? That's the confectionery; it's closed now but it's going to be reopened in a short while and I'm going to compete for the night life in this county, the after-the-movies trade. I'm going to serve setups in there and I'm going to redecorate. I got it all planned. [*She is talking eagerly now, as if to herself.*] Artificial branches of fruit trees in flower on the walls and ceilings!—It's going to be like an orchard in the spring!—My father, he had an orchard on Moon Lake. He made a wine garden of it. We had fifteen little white arbors with tables in them and they were covered with—grapevines and—we sold Dago red wine an' bootleg whiskey and beer. —They burned it up! My father was burned up in it. . . .

[JABE *knocks above more loudly and a hoarse voice shouts* "Lady!" *Figure appears at the door and calls:* "Mrs. Torrance?"]

Oh, that's the sandman with my sleeping tablets. [*Crosses to door.*] Thanks, Mr. Dubinsky, sorry I had to disturb you, sorry I—

[*Man mutters something and goes. She closes the door.*]

Well, go to hell, then, old bastard. . . . [*Returns with package.*]—You ever have trouble sleeping?

39

VAL: I can sleep or not sleep as long or short as I want to.

LADY: Is that right?

VAL: I can sleep on a concrete floor or go without sleeping, without even feeling sleepy, for forty-eight hours. And I can hold my breath three minutes without blacking out; I made ten dollars betting I could do it and I did it! And I can go a whole day without passing water.

LADY [*startled*]: Is *that* a *fact?*

VAL [*very simply as if he'd made an ordinary remark*]: That's a fact. I served time on a chain gang for vagrancy once and they tied me to a post all day and I stood there all day without passing water to show the sons of bitches that I could do it.

LADY:—I see what that auto repair man was talking about when he said this boy is a peculiar talker! Well—what else can you do? Tell me some more about your self-control!

VAL [*grinning*]: Well, they say that a woman can burn a man down. But I can burn down a woman.

LADY: Which woman?

VAL: Any two-footed woman.

LADY [*throws back her head in sudden friendly laughter as he grins at her with the simple candor of a child*]:—Well, there's lots of two-footed women round here that might be willin' to test the truth of that statement.

VAL: I'm saying I could. I'm not saying I would.

LADY: Don't worry, boy. I'm one two-footed woman that you don't have to convince of your perfect controls.

VAL: No, I'm done with all that.

LADY: What's the matter? Have they tired you out?

VAL: I'm not tired. I'm disgusted.

40

LADY: Aw, you're disgusted, huh?

VAL: I'm telling you, Lady, there's people bought and sold in this world like carcasses of hogs in butcher shops!

LADY: You ain't tellin' me nothin' I don't know.

VAL: You might think there's many and many kinds of people in this world but, Lady, there's just two kinds of people, the ones that are bought and the buyers! No!—there's one other kind . . .

LADY: What kind's that?

VAL: The kind that's never been branded.

LADY: You will be, man.

VAL: They got to catch me first.

LADY: Well, then, you better not settle down in this county.

VAL: You know they's a kind of bird that don't have legs so it can't light on nothing but has to stay all its life on its wings in the sky? That's true. I seen one once, it had died and fallen to earth and it was light-blue colored and its body was tiny as your little finger, that's the truth, it had a body as tiny as your little finger and so light on the palm of your hand it didn't weigh more than a feather, but its wings spread out this wide but they was transparent, the color of the sky and you could see through them. That's what they call protection coloring. Camouflage, they call it. You can't tell those birds from the sky and that's why the hawks don't catch them, don't see them up there in the high blue sky near the sun!

LADY: How about in gray weather?

VAL: They fly so high in gray weather the Goddam hawks would get dizzy. But those little birds, they don't have no legs at all and they live their whole lives on the wing, and they sleep on the wind, that's how they sleep at night, they just

41

spread their wings and go to sleep on the wind like other birds fold their wings and go to sleep on a tree. . . . [*Music fades in.*]—They sleep on the wind and . . . [*His eyes grow soft and vague and he lifts his guitar and accompanies the very faint music.*]—never light on this earth but one time when they die!

LADY:—I'd like to be one of those birds.

VAL: So'd I like to be one of those birds; they's lots of people would like to be one of those birds and never be— corrupted!

LADY: If one of those birds ever dies and falls on the ground and you happen to find it, I wish you would show it to me because I think maybe you just imagine there is a bird of that kind in existence. Because I don't think nothing living has ever been that free, not even nearly. Show me one of them birds and I'll say, Yes, God's made one perfect creature!—I sure would give this mercantile store and every bit of stock in it to be that tiny bird the color of the sky . . . for one night to sleep on the wind and—float!—around under th'—stars . . .

[JABE *knocks on floor.* LADY'S *eyes return to* VAL.]

—Because I sleep with a son of a bitch who bought me at a fire sale, and not in fifteen years have I had a single good dream, not one—oh!—*Shit* . . . I don't know why I'm— telling a stranger—this. . . . [*She rings the cashbox open.*] Take this dollar and go eat at the Al-Nite on the highway and come back here in the morning and I'll put you to work. I'll break you in clerking here and when the new confectionery opens, well, maybe I can use you in there.—That door locks when you close it!—But let's get one thing straight.

VAL: What thing?

LADY: I'm not interested in your perfect functions, in fact you don't interest me no more than the air that you stand in.

If that's understood we'll have a good working relation, but otherwise trouble!—Of course I know you're crazy, but they's lots of crazier people than you are still running loose and some of them in high positions, too. Just remember. No monkey business with me. Now go. Go eat, you're hungry.

VAL: Mind if I leave this here? My life's companion? [*He means his guitar.*]

LADY: Leave it here if you want to.

VAL: Thanks, Lady.

LADY: Don't mention it.

[*He crosses toward the door as a dog barks with passionate clarity in the distance. He turns to smile back at her and says:*]

VAL: I don't know nothing about you except you're nice but you are just about the nicest person that I have ever run into! And I'm going to be steady and honest and hard-working to please you and any time you have any more trouble sleeping, I know how to fix that for you. A lady osteopath taught me how to make little adjustments in the neck and spine that give you sound, natural sleep. Well, g'night, now.

[*He goes out. Count five. Then she throws back her head and laughs as lightly and gaily as a young girl. Then she turns and wonderingly picks up and runs her hands tenderly over his guitar as the curtain falls.*]

43

The store, afternoon, a few weeks later. The table and chair are back in the confectionery. LADY *is hanging up the phone.* VAL *is standing just outside the door. He turns and enters. Outside on the highway a mule team is laboring to pull a big truck back on the icy pavement. A Negro's voice shouts: "Hyyyyyyyyy-up."*

VAL [*moving to R. window*]: One a them big Diamond T trucks an' trailors gone off the highway last night and a six mule team is tryin' t' pull it back on. . . . [*He looks out window.*]

LADY [*coming from behind to R. of counter*]: Mister, we just now gotten a big fat complaint about you from a woman that says if she wasn't a widow her husband would come in here and beat the tar out of you.

VAL [*taking a step toward her*]: Yeah?—Is this a small pink-headed woman?

LADY: *Pin*-headed woman did you say?

VAL: Naw, I said, "Pink!"—A little pink-haired woman, in a checkered coat with pearl buttons this big on it.

LADY: I talked to her on the phone. She didn't go into such details about her appearance but she did say you got familiar. I said, "How? by his talk or behavior?" And she said, "Both!" —Now I was afraid of this when I warned you last week, "No monkey business here, boy!"

VAL: This little pink-headed woman bought a valentine from me and all I said is my *name* is Valentine to her. Few minutes later a small colored boy come in and delivered the valentine to me with something wrote on it an' I believe I still got it. . . . [*Finds and shows it to* LADY *who goes to him.*

LADY *reads it, and tears it fiercely to pieces. He lights a cigarette.*]

LADY: Signed it with a lipstick kiss? You didn't show up for this date?

VAL: No, ma'am. That's why she complained. [*Throws match on floor.*]

LADY: Pick that match up off the floor.

VAL: Are you bucking for sergeant, or something?

[*He throws match out the door with elaborate care. Her eyes follow his back.* VAL *returns lazily toward her.*]

LADY: Did you walk around in front of her that way?

VAL [*at counter*]: What way?

LADY: Slew-foot, slew-foot!

[*He regards her closely with good-humored perplexity.*]

Did you stand in front of her like that? That close? In that, that—*position?*

VAL: What position?

LADY: Ev'rything you do is suggestive!

VAL: Suggestive of what?

LADY: Of what you said you was through with—somethin' —*Oh, shoot, you know what I mean.*—Why'd 'ya think I give you a plain, dark business suit to work in?

VAL [*sadly*]: Un-hun. . . . [*Sighs and removes his blue jacket.*]

LADY: Now what're you takin' that off for?

VAL: I'm giving the suit back to you. I'll change my pants in the closet. [*Gives her the jacket and crosses into alcove.*]

45

LADY: Hey! I'm sorry! You hear me? I didn't sleep well last night. Hey! I said I'm sorry! You hear me? [*She enters alcove and returns immediately with* VAL'S *guitar and crosses to D.R. He follows.*]

VAL: Le' me have my guitar, Lady. You find too many faults with me and I tried to do good.

LADY: I told you I'm sorry. You want me to get down and lick the dust off your shoes?

VAL: Just give me back my guitar.

LADY: I ain't dissatisfied with you. I'm pleased with you, sincerely!

VAL: You sure don't show it.

LADY: My nerves are all shot to pieces. [*Extends hand to him.*] Shake.

VAL: You mean I ain't fired, so I don't have to quit?

[*They shake hands like two men. She hands him guitar—then silence falls between them.*]

LADY: You see, we don't know each other, we're, we're—just gettin'—acquainted.

VAL: That's right, like a couple of animals sniffin' around each other. . . .

[*The image embarrasses her. He crosses to counter, leans over and puts guitar behind it.*]

LADY: Well, not exactly like that, but—!

VAL: We don't know each other. How do people get to know each other? I used to think they did it by touch.

LADY: By what?

VAL: By touch, by touchin' each other.

LADY [*moving up and sitting on shoe-fitting chair which has been moved to R. window*]: Oh, you mean by close—contact!

VAL: But later it seemed like that made them more strangers than ever, uhh, huh, more strangers than ever. . . .

LADY: Then how d'you think they get to know each other?

VAL [*sitting on counter*]: Well, in answer to your last question, I would say this: Nobody ever gets to know *no body!* We're all of us sentenced to solitary confinement inside our own skins, for life! You understand me, Lady?—I'm tellin' you it's the truth, we got to face it, we're under a life-long sentence to solitary confinement inside our own lonely skins for as long as we live on this earth!

LADY [*rising and crossing to him*]: Oh, no, I'm not a big optimist but I cannot agree with something as sad as that statement!

[*They are sweetly grave as two children; the store is somewhat dusky. She sits in chair R. of counter.*]

VAL: *Listen!*—When I was a kid on Witches Bayou? After my folks all scattered away like loose chicken's feathers blown around by the wind?—I stayed there alone on the bayou, hunted and trapped out of season and hid from the law!—*Listen!*—All that time, all that lonely time, I felt I was—waiting for something!

LADY: What for?

VAL: What does anyone wait for? For something to happen, for anything to happen, to make things make more sense. . . . It's hard to remember what that feeling was like because I've lost it now, but I was waiting for something like if you ask a question you wait for someone to answer, but you ask the wrong question or you ask the wrong person and the answer don't come.

47

Does everything stop because you don't get the answer? No, it goes right on as if the answer was given, day comes after day and night comes after night, and you're still waiting for someone to answer the question and going right on as if the question was answered. And then—well—then. . . .

LADY: Then what?

VAL: You get the make-believe answer.

LADY: What answer is that?

VAL: Don't pretend you don't know because you do!

LADY:—Love?

VAL [*placing hand on her shoulder*]: That's the make-believe answer. It's fooled many a fool besides you an' me, that's the God's truth, Lady, and you had better believe it.

[LADY *looks reflectively at* VAL *and he goes on speaking and sits on stool below counter.*]

—I met a girl on the bayou when I was fourteen. I'd had a feeling that day that if I just kept poling the boat down the bayou a little bit further I would come bang into whatever it was I'd been so long expecting!

LADY: Was she the answer, this girl that you met on the bayou?

VAL: She made me think that she was.

LADY: How did she do that?

VAL: By coming out on the dogtrot of a cabin as naked as I was in that flat-bottom boat! She stood there a while with the daylight burning around her as bright as heaven as far as I could see. You seen the inside of a shell, how white that is, pearly white? Her naked skin was like that.—Oh, God, I remember a bird flown out of the moss and its wings made a shadow on her, and then it sung a single, high clear note,

48

and as if she was waiting for that as a kind of a signal to catch me, she turned and smiled, and walked on back in the cabin. . . .

LADY: You followed?

VAL: Yes, I followed, I followed, like a bird's tail follows a bird, I followed!

I thought that she give me the answer to the question, I'd been waiting for, but afterwards I wasn't sure that was it, but from that time the question wasn't much plainer than the answer and—

LADY:—What?

VAL: At fifteen I left Witches Bayou. When the dog died I sold my boat and the gun. . . . I went to New Orleans in this snakeskin jacket. . . . It didn't take long for me to learn the score.

LADY: What did you learn?

VAL: I learned that I had something to sell besides snake-skins and other wild things' skins I caught on the bayou. I was corrupted! That's the answer. . . .

LADY: Naw, that ain't the answer!

VAL: Okay, *you* tell me the answer!

LADY: I don't know the answer, I just know corruption ain't the answer. I know that much. If I thought that was the answer I'd take Jabe's pistol or his morphine tablets and—

[*A woman bursts into store.*]

WOMAN: I got to use your pay-phone!

LADY: Go ahead. Help yourself.

[*Woman crosses to phone, deposits coin.* LADY *crosses to confectionery. To* VAL:]

Get me a coke from the cooler.

[VAL *crosses and goes out R. During the intense activity among the choral women,* LADY *and* VAL *seem bemused as if they were thinking back over their talk before. For the past minute or two a car horn has been heard blowing repeatedly in the near distance.*]

WOMAN [*at phone*]: Cutrere place, get me the Cutrere place, will yuh? David Cutrere or his wife, whichever comes to the phone!

[BEULAH *rushes in from the street to R.C.*]

BEULAH: Lady, Lady, where's Lady! Carol Cutrere is—!

WOMAN: Quiet, please! I am callin' her brother about her!

[LADY *sits at table in confectionery.*]

[*At phone:*] Who's this I'm talking to? Good! I'm calling about your sister, Carol Cutrere. She is blowing her car horn at the Red Crown station, she is blowing and blowing her car horn at the Red Crown station because my husband give the station attendants instructions not to service her car, and she is blowing and blowing and blowing on her horn, drawing a big crowd there and, Mr. Cutrere, I thought that you and your father had agreed to keep that girl out of Two River County for good, that's what we all understood around here.

[*Car horn.*]

BEULAH [*Listening with excited approval*]: Good! Good! Tell him that if—

[DOLLY *enters.*]

DOLLY: She's gotten out of the car and—

BEULAH: *Shhh!*

WOMAN: Well, I just wanted to let you know she's back here in town makin' another disturbance and my husband's on the phone now at the Red Crown station—

[DOLLY *goes outside and looks off.*]

trying to get the Sheriff, so if she gits picked up again by th' law, you can't say I didn't warn you, Mr. Cutrere.

[*Car horn.*]

DOLLY [*coming back in*]: *Oh, good! Good!*

BEULAH: Where is she, where's she gone now?

WOMAN: You better be quick about it. Yes, I do. I sympathize with you and your father and with Mrs. Cutrere, but Carol cannot demand service at our station, we just refuse to wait on her, she's not—Hello? Hello? [*She jiggles phone violently.*]

BEULAH: What's he doin'? Comin' to pick her up?

DOLLY: Call the Sheriff's office!

[BEULAH *goes outside again.* VAL *comes back with a bottle of Coca-Cola—hands it to* LADY *and leans on juke box.*]

[*Going out to* BEULAH] What's goin' on now?

BEULAH [*outside*]: Look, look, they're pushing her out of the station driveway.

[*They forget* LADY *in this new excitement. Ad libs continual. The short woman from the station charges back out of the store.*]

DOLLY: Where is Carol?

BEULAH: Going into the White Star Pharmacy!

[DOLLY *rushes back in to the phone.*]

BEULAH [*crossing to* LADY]: Lady, I want you to give me your word that if that Cutrere girl comes in here, you won't wait on her! You hear me?

LADY: No.

BEULAH:—What? Will you refuse to wait on her?

51

LADY: I can't refuse to wait on anyone in this store.

BEULAH: Well, I'd like to know why you can't.

DOLLY: Shhh! I'm on the phone!

BEULAH: Who you phonin' Dolly?

DOLLY: That White Star Pharmacy! I want to make sure that Mr. Dubinsky refuses to wait on that girl! [*Having found and deposited coin*] I want the White Far Starmacy. I mean the—[*Stamps foot*]—White Star Pharmacy!—I'm so upset my tongue's twisted!

[LADY *hands coke to* VAL. BEULAH *is at the window.*]

I'm getting a busy signal. Has she come out yet?

BEULAH: No, she's still in the White Star!

DOLLY: Maybe they're not waiting on her.

BEULAH: Dubinsky'd wait on a purple-bottom baboon if it put a dime on th' counter an' pointed at something!

DOLLY: I know she sat at a table in the Blue Bird Café half'n hour last time she was here and the waitresses never came near her!

BEULAH: That's different. They're not foreigners there!

[DOLLY *crosses to counter.*]

You can't ostracize a person out of this county unless everybody cooperates. Lady just told me that she was going to wait on her if she comes here.

DOLLY: Lady wouldn't do that.

BEULAH: *Ask* her! She told *me* she would!

LADY [*rising and turning at once to the women and shouting at them*]: Oh, for God's sake, no! I'm not going to refuse to wait on her because you all don't like her! Besides I'm delighted that wild girl is givin' her brother so much trouble! [*After this outburst she goes back of the counter.*]

DOLLY [*at phone*]: Hush! Mr. Dubinsky! This is Dolly Hamma, Mr. "Dog" Hamma's wife!

[CAROL *quietly enters the front door.*]

I want to ask you, is Carol Cutrere in your drugstore?

BEULAH [*warningly*]: Dolly!

CAROL: No. She isn't.

DOLLY:—What?

CAROL: She's here.

[BEULAH *goes into confectionery.* CAROL *moves toward* VAL *to D.R.C.*]

DOLLY:—Aw!—Never mind, Mr. Dubinsky, I—[*Hangs up furiously and crosses to door.*]

[*A silence in which they all stare at the girl from various positions about the store. She has been on the road all night in an open car: her hair is blown wild, her face flushed and eyes bright with fever. Her manner in the scene is that of a wild animal at bay, desperate but fearless.*]

LADY [*finally and quietly*]: Hello, Carol.

CAROL: Hello, Lady.

LADY [*defiantly cordial*]: I thought that you were in New Orleans, Carol.

CAROL: Yes, I was. Last night.

LADY: Well, you got back fast.

CAROL: I drove all night.

LADY: In that storm?

CAROL: The wind took the top off my car but I didn't stop.

53

[*She watches* VAL *steadily; he steadily ignores her; turns away and puts bottles of Coca-Cola on a table.*]

LADY [*with growing impatience*]: Is something wrong at home, is someone sick?

CAROL [*absently*]: No. No, not that I know of, I wouldn't know if there was, they—may I sit down?

LADY: Why, sure.

CAROL [*crossing to chair at counter and sitting*]:—They pay me to stay away so I wouldn't know. . . .

[*Silence.* VAL *walks deliberately past her and goes into alcove.*]

—I think I have a fever, I feel like I'm catching pneumonia, everything's so far away. . . .

[*Silence again except for the faint, hissing whispers of* BEULAH *and* DOLLY *at the back of the store.*]

LADY [*with a touch of exasperation*]: Is there something you want?

CAROL: Everything seems miles away. . . .

LADY: Carol, I said is there anything you want here?

CAROL: Excuse me!—yes. . . .

LADY: Yes, what?

CAROL: Don't bother now. I'll wait.

[VAL *comes out of alcove with the blue jacket on.*]

LADY: Wait for what, what are you waiting for! You don't have to wait for nothing, just say what you want and if I got it in stock I'll give it to you!

[*Phone rings once.*]

CAROL [*vaguely*]:—Thank you—no. . . .

54

LADY [*to* VAL]: Get that phone, Val.

[DOLLY *crosses and hisses something inaudible to* BEULAH.]

BEULAH [*rising*]: I just want to wait here to see if she does or she don't.

DOLLY: She just said she would!

BEULAH: Just the same, I'm gonna wait!!

VAL [*at phone*]: Yes, sir, she is.—I'll tell her. [*Hangs up and speaks to* LADY:] Her brother's heard she's here and he's coming to pick her up.

LADY: *David Cutrere is not coming in this store!*

DOLLY: Aw-aw!

BEULAH: David Cutrere used to be her lover.

DOLLY: I remember you told me.

LADY [*wheels about suddenly toward the women*]: Beulah! Dolly! Why're you back there hissing together like geese? [*Coming from behind counter to R.C.*] Why don't you go to th'—Blue Bird and—have some hot coffee—talk there!

BEULAH: It looks like we're getting what they call the bum's rush.

DOLLY: I never stay where I'm not wanted and when I'm not wanted somewhere I never come back!

[*They cross out and slam door.*]

LADY [*after a pause*]: What did you come here for?

CAROL: To deliver a message.

LADY: To me?

CAROL: No.

LADY: Then who?

55

[CAROL *stares at* LADY *gravely a moment, then turns slowly to look at* VAL.]

—Him?—Him?

[CAROL *nods slowly and slightly.*]

OK, then, give him the message, deliver the message to him.

CAROL: It's a private message. Could I speak to him alone, please?

[LADY *gets a shawl from a hook.*]

LADY: Oh, for God's sake! Your brother's plantation is ten minutes from here in that sky-blue Cadillac his rich wife give him. Now look, he's on his way here but I won't let him come in, I don't even want his hand to touch the door-handle. I know your message, this boy knows your message, there's nothing private about it. But I tell you, that this boy's not for sale in my store!—Now—I'm going out to watch for the sky-blue Cadillac on the highway. When I see it, I'm going to throw this door open and holler and when I holler, I want you out of this door like a shot from a pistol!—that fast! Understand?

[NOTE: *Above scene is overextended. This can be remedied by a very lively performance. It might also help to indicate a division between the Lady-Val scene and the group scene that follows.*]

[LADY *slams door behind her. The loud noise of the door-slam increases the silence that follows.* VAL'S *oblivious attitude is not exactly hostile, but deliberate. There's a kind of purity in it; also a kind of refusal to concern himself with a problem that isn't his own. He holds his guitar with a specially tender concentration, and strikes a soft chord on it. The girl stares at* VAL; *he whistles a note and tightens a guitar string to the pitch of the whistle, not looking at*

56

*the girl. Since this scene is followed by the emotional scene
between* LADY *and* DAVID, *it should be keyed somewhat
lower than written; it's important that* VAL *should not seem
brutal in his attitude toward* CAROL; *there should be an air
between them of two lonely children.*]

VAL [*in a soft, preoccupied tone*]: You told the lady I work
for that you had a message for me. Is that right, Miss? Have
you got a message for me?

CAROL [*she rises, moves a few steps toward him, hesitantly.*
VAL *whistles, plucks guitar string, changes pitch*]: You've
spilt some ashes on your new blue suit.

VAL: Is that the message?

CAROL [*moves away a step*]: No. No, that was just an
excuse to touch you. The message is—

VAL: What?

[*Music fades in—guitar.*]

CAROL:—I'd love to hold something the way you hold your
guitar, that's how I'd love to hold something, with such—
tender protection! I'd love to hold *you* that way, with that
same *tender protection!* [*Her hand has fallen onto his knee,
which he has drawn up to rest a foot on the counter stool.*]—
Because you hang the moon for me!

VAL [*he speaks to her, not roughly but in a tone that holds
a long history that began with a romantic acceptance of such
declarations as she has just made to him, and that turned
gradually to his present distrust. He puts guitar down and
goes to her*]: Who're you tryin' t' fool beside you'self? You
couldn't stand the weight of a man's body on you. [*He
casually picks up her wrist and pushes the sleeve back from
it.*] What's this here? A human wrist with a bone? It feels
like a twig I could snap with two fingers. . . . [*Gently, negli-*

57

gently, pushes collar of her trench coat back from her bare throat and shoulders. Runs a finger along her neck tracing a vein.] Little girl, you're transparent, I can see the veins in you. A man's weight on you would break you like a bundle of sticks. . . .

[*Music fades out.*]

CAROL [*gazes at him, startled by his perception*]: Isn't it funny! You've hit on the truth about me. The act of love-making is almost unbearably painful, and yet, of course, I do bear it, because to be not alone, even for a few moments, is worth the pain and the danger. It's dangerous for me because I'm not built for childbearing.

VAL: Well, then, fly away, little bird, fly away before you—get broke. [*He turns back to his guitar.*]

CAROL: Why do you dislike me?

VAL [*turning back*]: I never dislike nobody till they interfere with me.

CAROL: How have I interfered with you? Did I snitch when I saw my cousin's watch on you?

VAL [*Beginning to remove his watch*]:—You won't take my word for a true thing I told you. I'm thirty years old and I'm done with the crowd you run with and the places you run to. The Club Rendezvous, the Starlite Lounge, the Music Bar, and all the night places. Here—[*Offers watch*]—take this Rolex Chronometer that tells the time of the day and the day of the week and the month and all the crazy moon's phases. I never stole nothing before. When I stole that I known it was time for me to get off the party, so take it back, now, to Bertie. . . . [*He takes her hand and tries to force the watch into her fist. There is a little struggle, he can't open her fist. She is crying, but staring fiercely into his eyes.*

58

He draws a hissing breath and hurls watch violently across the floor.]

—That's my message to you and the pack you run with!

CAROL [*flinging coat away*]: *I RUN WITH NOBODY!*

—I hoped I could run with you. . . . [*Music stops short.*] You're in danger here, Snakeskin. You've taken off the jacket that said: "I'm wild, I'm alone!" and put on the nice blue uniform of a convict! . . . Last night I woke up thinking about you again. I drove all night to bring you this warning of danger. . . . [*Her trembling hand covers her lips.*]—The message I came here to give you was a warning of danger! I hoped you'd hear me and let me take you away before it's —too late.

[*Door bursts open.* LADY *rushes inside, crying out:*]

LADY: *Your brother's coming, go out! He can't come in!*

[CAROL *picks up coat and goes into confectionery, sobbing.* VAL *crosses toward door.*]

Lock that door! Don't let him come in my store!

[CAROL *sinks sobbing at table.* LADY *runs up to the landing of the stairs as* DAVID CUTRERE *enters the store. He is a tall man in hunter's clothes. He is hardly less handsome now than he was in his youth but something has gone: his power is that of a captive who rules over other captives. His face, his eyes, have something of the same desperate, unnatural hardness that* LADY *meets the world with.*]

DAVID: Carol?

VAL: She's in there. [*He nods toward the dim confectionery into which the girl has retreated.*]

DAVID [*crossing*]: Carol!

[*She rises and advances a few steps into the lighted area of the stage.*]

59

You broke the agreement.

[CAROL *nods slightly, staring at* VAL.]

[*Harshly:*] All right. I'll drive you back. Where's your coat?

[CAROL *murmurs something inaudible, staring at* VAL.]

Where is her coat, where is my sister's coat?

[VAL *crosses below and picks up the coat that* CAROL *has dropped on the floor and hands it to* DAVID. *He throws it roughly about* CAROL'S *shoulders and propels her forcefully toward the store entrance.* VAL *moves away to D.R.*]

LADY [*suddenly and sharply*]: Wait, please!

[DAVID *looks up at the landing; stands frozen as* LADY *rushes down the stairs.*]

DAVID [*softly, hoarsely*]: How—*are* you, Lady?

LADY [*turning to* VAL]: Val, go out.

DAVID [*to* CAROL]: Carol, will you wait for me in my car?

[*He opens the door for his sister; she glances back at* VAL *with desolation in her eyes.* VAL *crosses quickly through the confectionery. Sound of door closing in there.* CAROL *nods slightly as if in sad response to some painful question and goes out of the store. Pause.*]

LADY: I told you once to never come in this store.

DAVID: I came for my sister. . . . [*He turns as if to go.*]

LADY: No, wait!

DAVID: I don't dare leave my sister alone on the road.

LADY: I have something to tell you I never told you before. [*She crosses to him.* DAVID *turns back to her, then moves away to D.R.C.*]

—I—carried your child in my body the summer you quit me.

[*Silence.*]

DAVID:—I—didn't know.

LADY: No, no, I didn't write you no letter about it; I was proud then; I had pride. But I had your child in my body the summer you quit me, that summer they burned my father in his wine garden, and you, you washed your hands clean of any connection with a Dago bootlegger's daughter and—[*Her breathless voice momentarily falters and she makes a fierce gesture as she struggles to speak.*]—took that—society girl that—restored your homeplace and give you such—[*Catches breath.*]—wellborn children. . . .

DAVID:—I—didn't know.

LADY: Well, now you do know, you know now. I carried your child in my body the summer you quit me but I had it cut out of my body, and they cut my heart out with it!

DAVID:—I—didn't know.

LADY: I wanted death after that, but death don't come when you *want* it, it comes when you don't want it! I wanted death, then, but I took the next best thing. *You* sold *yourself. I* sold *my* self. *You* was bought. *I* was bought. You made whores of us both!

DAVID:—I—didn't know. . . .

[*Mandolin, barely audible, "Dicitincello Voie."*]

LADY: But that's all a long time ago. Some reason I drove by there a few nights ago; the shore of the lake where my father had his wine garden? You remember? You remember the wine garden of my father?

[DAVID *stares at her. She turns away.*]

No, you don't? You don't remember it even?

DAVID:—Lady, I don't—remember—anything else. . . .

LADY: The mandolin of my father, the songs that I sang with my father in my father's wine garden?

DAVID: Yes, I don't remember anything else. . . .

LADY: *Core Ingrata! Come Le Rose!* And we disappeared and he would call, "Lady? Lady?" *[Turns to him.] How could I answer him with two tongues in my mouth! [A sharp hissing intake of breath, eyes opened wide, hand clapped over her mouth as if what she said was unendurable to her. He turns instantly, sharply away.]*

> *[Music stops short.* JABE *begins to knock for her on the floor above. She crosses to stairs, stops, turns.]*

I hold hard feelings!—Don't ever come here again. If your wild sister comes here, send somebody else for her, not you, not you. Because I hope never to feel this knife again in me. *[Her hand is on her chest; she breathes with difficulty.]*

> *[He turns away from her; starts toward the door. She takes a step toward him.]*

And don't pity me neither. I haven't gone down so terribly far in the world. I got a going concern in this mercantile store, in there's the confectionery which'll reopen this spring, it's being done over to make it the place that all the young people will come to, it's going to be like—

> *[He touches the door, pauses with his back to her.]*

—the wine garden of my father, those wine-drinking nights when you had something better than anything you've had since!

DAVID: Lady—*That's*—

LADY:—*What?*

DAVID:—*True!* [*Opens door.*]

LADY: Go now. I just wanted to tell you my life ain't over.

[*He goes out as* JABE *continues knocking. She stands, stunned, motionless till* VAL *quietly re-enters the store. She becomes aware of his return rather slowly; then she murmurs:*]

I made a fool of myself. . . .

VAL: What?

[*She crosses to stairs.*]

LADY: *I made a fool of myself!*

[*She goes up the stairs with effort as the lights change slowly to mark a division of scenes.*]

Sunset of that day. VAL *is alone in the store, as if preparing to go. The sunset is fiery. A large woman opens the door and stands there looking dazed. It is* VEE TALBOTT.

VAL [*turning*]: Hello, Mrs. Talbott.

VEE: Something's gone wrong with my eyes. I can't see nothing.

VAL [*going to her*]: Here, let me help you. You probably drove up here with that setting sun in your face. [*Leading her to shoe-fitting chair at R. window.*] There now. Set down right here.

VEE: Thank you—so—much. . . .

VAL: I haven't seen you since that night you brought me here to ask for this job.

VEE: Has the minister called on you yet? Reverend Tooker? I made him promise he would. I told him you were new around here and weren't affiliated to any church yet. I want you to go to ours.

VAL:—That's—mighty kind of you.

VEE: The Church of the Resurrection, it's Episcopal.

VAL: Uh, huh.

VEE: Unwrap that picture, please.

VAL: Sure. [*He tears paper off canvas.*]

VEE: It's the Church of the Resurrection. I give it a sort of imaginative treatment. You know, Jabe and Lady have never darkened a church door. I thought it ought to be hung where Jabe could look at it, it might help to bring that poor dying man to Jesus. . . .

[VAL *places it against chair* R. *of counter and crouches before the canvas, studying it long and seriously.* VEE *coughs nervously, gets up, bends to look at the canvas, sits uncertainly back down.* VAL *smiles at her warmly, then back to the canvas.*]

VAL [*at last*]: What's this here in the picture?

VEE: The steeple.

VAL: Aw.—Is the church steeple red?

VEE: Why—no, but—

VAL: Why'd you paint it red, then?

VEE: Oh, well, you see, I—[*Laughs nervously, childlike in her growing excitement.*]—I just, just *felt* it that way! I paint a thing how I feel it instead of always the way it actually is. Appearances are misleading, nothing is what it looks like to the eyes. You got to have—*vision—to see!*

VAL:—Yes. Vision. Vision!—to see. . . . [*Rises, nodding gravely, emphatically.*]

VEE: I paint from vision. They call me a visionary.

VAL: Oh.

VEE [*with shy pride*]: That's what the New Orleans and Memphis newspaper people admire so much in my work. They call it a primitive style, the work of a visionary. One of my pictures is hung on the exhibition in Audubon Park museum and they have asked for others. I can't turn them out fast enough!—I have to wait for—visions, no, I—I can't paint without—visions . . . I couldn't *live* without visions!

VAL: Have you always had visions?

VEE: No, just since I was born, I—[*Stops short, startled by the absurdity of her answer. Both laugh suddenly, then she rushes on, her great bosom heaving with curious excitement,*

65

twisting in her chair, gesturing with clenched hands.] I was born, I was born with a caul! A sort of thing like a veil, a thin, thin sort of a web was over my eyes. They call that a caul. It's a sign that you're going to have visions, and I did, I had them! [*Pauses for breath; light fades.*]—When I was little my baby sister died. Just one day old, she died. They had to baptize her at midnight to save her soul.

VAL: Uh-huh. [*He sits opposite her, smiling, attentive.*]

VEE: The minister came at midnight, and after the baptism service, he handed the bowl of holy water to me and told me, "Be sure to empty this out on the ground!"—I didn't. I was scared to go out at midnight, with, with—death! in the— house and—I sneaked into the kitchen; I emptied the holy water into the kitchen sink—thunder struck!—the kitchen sink turned black, the kitchen sink turned absolutely black!

[SHERIFF TALBOTT *enters the front door.*]

TALBOTT: Mama! What're you doin'?

VEE: Talkin'.

TALBOTT: I'm gonna see Jabe a minute, you go out and wait in th' car. [*He goes up. She rises slowly, picks up canvas and moves to counter.*]

VEE:—Oh, I—tell you!—since I got into this painting, my whole outlook is different. I can't explain how it is, the differ- ence to me.

VAL: You don't have to explain. I know what you mean. Before you started to paint, it didn't make sense.

VEE:—What—what didn't?

VAL: Existence!

VEE [*slowly and softly*]: No—no, it didn't . . . existence didn't make sense. . . . [*She places canvas on guitar on counter and sits in chair.*]

66

VAL [*rising and crossing to her*]: You lived in Two River County, the wife of the county Sheriff. You saw awful things take place.

VEE: Awful! Things!

VAL: Beatings!

VEE: Yes!

VAL: Lynchings!

VEE: Yes!

VAL: Runaway convicts torn to pieces by hounds!

[*This is the first time she could express this horror.*]

VEE: *Chain-gang dogs!*

VAL: Yeah?

VEE: Tear fugitives!

VAL: Yeah?

VEE:—to *pieces.* . . .

[*She had half risen: now sinks back faintly.* VAL *looks beyond her in the dim store, his light eyes have a dark gaze. It may be that his speech is too articulate: counteract this effect by groping, hesitations.*]

VAL [*moving away a step*]: But violence ain't quick always. Sometimes it's slow. Some tornadoes are slow. Corruption—rots men's hearts and—rot is slow. . . .

VEE:—How do you—?

VAL: Know? I been a witness, I know!

VEE: *I* been a witness! *I* know!

VAL: We seen these things from seats down front at the show. [*He crouches before her and touches her hands in her lap. Her breath shudders.*] And so you begun to paint your

67

visions. Without no plan, no training, you started to paint as if God touched your fingers. [*He lifts her hands slowly, gently from her soft lap.*] You made some beauty out of this dark country with these two, soft, woman hands. . . .

[TALBOTT *appears on the stair landing, looks down, silent.*] Yeah, you made some beauty! [*Strangely, gently, he lifts her hands to his mouth. She gasps.* TALBOTT *calls out:*]

TALBOTT: *Hey!*

[VEE *springs up, gasping.*]

[*Descending*] *Cut this crap!*

[VAL *moves away to R.C.*]

[*To* VEE:] Go out. Wait in the car. [*He stares at* VAL *till* VEE *lumbers out as if dazed. After a while:*]

Jabe Torrance told me to take a good look at you. [*Crosses to* VAL.] Well, now, I've taken that look. [*Nods shortly. Goes out of store. The store is now very dim. As door closes on* TALBOTT, VAL *picks up painting; he goes behind counter and places it on a shelf, then picks up his guitar and sits on counter. Lights go down to mark a division as he sings and plays "Heavenly Grass."*]

As VAL *finishes the song,* LADY *descends the stair. He rises and turns on a green-shaded light bulb.*

VAL [*to* LADY]: You been up there a long time.

LADY:—I gave him morphine. He must be out of his mind. He says such awful things to me. He says I want him to die.

VAL: You sure you don't?

LADY: I don't want no one to die. Death's terrible, VAL.

[*Pause. She wanders to the front window R. He takes his guitar and crosses to the door.*] You gotta go now?

VAL: I'm late.

LADY: Late for what? You got a date with somebody?

VAL:—No. . . .

LADY: Then stay a while. Play something. I'm all unstrung. . . .

[*He crosses back and leans against counter; the guitar is barely audible, under the speeches.*]

I made a terrible fool of myself down here today with—

VAL:—That girl's brother?

LADY: Yes, I—threw away——pride. . . .

VAL: His sister said she'd come here to give me a warning. I wonder what of?

LADY [*sitting in shoe-fitting chair*]:—I said things to him I should of been too proud to say. . . .

[*Both are pursuing their own reflections; guitar continues softly.*]

VAL: Once or twice lately I've woke up with a fast heart, shouting something, and had to pick up my guitar to calm myself down. . . . Somehow or other I can't get used to this place, I don't feel safe in this place, but I—want to stay. . . .

[*Stops short; sound of wild baying.*]

LADY: The chain-gang dogs are chasing some runaway convict. . . .

VAL: *Run boy! Run fast, brother! If they catch you, you never will run again! That's*—[*He has thrust his guitar under his arm on this line and crossed to the door.*]—for sure. . . . [*The baying of the dogs changes, becomes almost a single savage note.*]—Uh-huh—the dogs've got him. . . . [*Pause.*] They're tearing him to pieces! [*Pause. Baying continues. A shot is fired. The baying dies out. He stops with his hand on the door; glances back at her; nods; draws the door open. The wind sings loud in the dusk.*]

LADY: *Wait!*

VAL:—Huh?

LADY:—Where do you stay?

VAL:—When?

LADY: Nights.

VAL: I stay at the Wildwood cabins on the highway.

LADY: You like it there?

VAL: Uh-huh.

LADY:—Why?

VAL: I got a comfortable bed, a two-burner stove, a shower and icebox there.

LADY: You want to save money?

VAL: I never could in my life.

LADY: You could if you stayed on the place.

VAL: What place?

LADY: This place.

VAL: Whereabouts on this place?

LADY [*pointing to alcove*]: Back of that curtain.

VAL:—Where they try on clothes?

LADY: There's a cot there. A nurse slept on it when Jabe had his first operation, and there's a washroom down here and I'll get a plumber to put in a hot an' cold shower! I'll—fix it up nice for you. . . . [*She rises, crosses to foot of stairs. Pause. He lets the door shut, staring at her.*]

VAL [*moving D.C.*]:—I—don't like to be—obligated.

LADY: There wouldn't be no obligation, you'd do me a favor. I'd feel safer at night with somebody on the place. I would; it would cost you nothing! And you could save up that money you spend on the cabin. How much? Ten a week? Why, two or three months from now you'd—save enough money to—[*Makes a wide gesture with a short laugh as if startled.*] Go on! Take a look at it! See if it don't suit you! —All right. . . .

[*But he doesn't move; he appears reflective.*]

LADY [*shivering, hugging herself*]: Where does heat go in this building?

VAL [*reflectively*]:—Heat rises. . . .

LADY: You with your dog's temperature, don't feel cold, do you? I do! I turn blue with it!

VAL:—Yeah. . . .

[*The wait is unendurable to* LADY.]

LADY: *Well, aren't you going to look at it, the room back there, and see if it suits you or not?!*

71

VAL:—I'll go and take a look at it. . . .

[*He crosses to the alcove and disappears behind the curtain. A light goes on behind it, making its bizarre pattern translucent: a gold tree with scarlet fruit and white birds in it, formally designed. Truck roars; lights sweep the frosted window.* LADY *gasps aloud; takes out a pint bottle and a glass from under the counter, setting them down with a crash that makes her utter a startled exclamation: then a startled laugh. She pours a drink and sits in chair R. of counter. The lights turn off behind the alcove curtain and* VAL *comes back out. She sits stiffly without looking at him as he crosses back lazily, goes behind counter, puts guitar down. His manner is gently sad as if he had met with a familiar, expected disappointment. He sits down quietly on edge of counter and takes the pint bottle and pours himself a shot of the liquor with a reflective sigh. Boards creak loudly, contracting with the cold.* LADY'S *voice is harsh and sudden, demanding:*]

LADY: *Well, is it okay or—what!*

VAL: I never been in a position where I could turn down something I got for nothing in my life. I like that picture in there. That's a famous picture, that "September Morn" picture you got on the wall in there. Ha ha! I might have trouble sleeping in a room with that picture. I might keep turning the light on to take another look at it! The way she's cold in that water and sort of crouched over in it, holding her body like that, that—might—ha ha!—sort of keep me awake. . . .

LADY: Aw, you with your dog's temperature and your control of all functions, it would take more than a picture to keep you awake!

VAL: I was just kidding.

LADY: I was just kidding too.

72

VAL: But you know how a single man is. He don't come home every night with just his shadow.

[*Pause. She takes a drink.*]

LADY: You bring girls home nights to the Wildwood cabins, do you?

VAL: I ain't so far. But I would like to feel free to. That old life is what I'm used to. I always worked nights in cities and if you work nights in cities you live in a different city from those that work days.

LADY: Yes. I know, I—imagine. . . .

VAL: The ones that work days in cities and the ones that work nights in cities, they live in different cities. The cities have the same name but they are different cities. As different as night and day. There's something wild in the country that only the night people know. . . .

LADY: Yeah, I know!

VAL: I'm thirty years old!—but sudden changes don't work, it takes—

LADY:—Time—yes. . . .

[*Slight pause which she finds disconcerting. He slides off counter and moves around below it.*]

VAL: You been good to me, Lady.—Why d'you want me to stay here?

LADY [*defensively*]: I told you why.

VAL: For company nights?

LADY: Yeah, to, to!—*guard the store,* nights!

VAL: To be a night watchman?

LADY: Yeah, to be a night *watchman.*

VAL: You feel nervous alone here?

73

LADY: Naturally now!—Jabe sleeps with a pistol next to him but if somebody broke in the store, he couldn't git up and all I could do is holler!—Who'd *hear* me? They got a telephone girl on the night shift with—sleepin' sickness, I think! Anyhow, why're you so suspicious? You look at me like you thought I was *plottin'*.—Kind people *exist*: Even me! [*She sits up rigid in chair, lips and eyes tight closed, drawing in a loud breath which comes from a tension both personal and vicarious.*]

VAL: I understand, Lady, but. . . . Why're you sitting up so stiff in that chair?

LADY: Ha! [*Sharp laugh; she leans back in chair.*]

VAL: You're still unrelaxed.

LADY: I know.

VAL: Relax. [*Moving around close to her.*] I'm going to show you some tricks I learned from a lady osteopath that took me in, too.

LADY: What tricks?

VAL: How to manipulate joints and bones in a way that makes you feel like a loose piece of string. [*Moves behind her chair. She watches him.*] Do you trust me or don't you?

LADY: Yeah, I trust you completely, but—

VAL: Well then, lean forward a little and raise your arms up and turn sideways in the chair.

[*She follows these instructions.*]

Drop your head. [*He manipulates her head and neck.*] Now the spine, Lady. [*He places his knee against the small of her backbone and she utters a sharp, startled laugh as he draws her backbone hard against his kneecap.*]

LADY: Ha, ha!—That makes a sound like, like, like!—boards contracting with cold in the building, ha, ha!

74

[*He relaxes.*]

VAL: Better?

LADY: Oh, yes!—much . . . thanks. . . .

VAL [*stroking her neck*]: Your skin is like silk. You're light skinned to be Italian.

LADY: Most people in this country think Italian people are dark. Some are but not all are! Some of them are fair . . . very fair. . . . My father's people were dark but my mother's people were fair. Ha ha!

[*The laughter is senseless. He smiles understandingly at her as she chatters to cover confusion. He turns away, then goes above and sits on counter close to her.*]

My mother's mother's sister—come here from Monte Cassino, to die, with relations!—but I think people always die alone . . . with or without relations. I was a little girl then and I remember it took her such a long, long time to die we almost forgot her.—And she was so quiet . . . in a corner. . . . And I remember asking her one time, Zia Teresa, how does it feel to die?—Only a little girl would ask such a question, ha ha! Oh, and I remember her answer. She said— "It's a lonely feeling."

I think she wished she had stayed in Italy and died in a place that she knew. . . . [*Looks at him directly for the first time since mentioning the alcove.*] Well, there is a washroom, and I'll get the plumber to put in a hot and cold shower! Well—[*Rises, retreats awkwardly from the chair. His interest seems to have wandered from her.*] I'll go up and get some clean linen and make up that bed in there.

[*She turns and walks rapidly, almost running, to stairs. He appears lost in some private reflection but as soon as she has disappeared above the landing, he says something under*] *his breath and crosses directly to the cashbox. He coughs loudly to cover the sound of ringing it open; scoops out a fistful of bills and coughs again to cover the sound of slamming drawer shut. Picks up his guitar and goes out the front door of store.* LADY *returns downstairs, laden with linen. The outer darkness moans through the door left open. She crosses to the door and a little outside it, peering both ways down the dark road. Then she comes in furiously, with an Italian curse, shutting the door with her foot or shoulder, and throws the linen down on counter. She crosses abruptly to cashbox, rings it open and discovers theft. Slams drawer violently shut.*]

Thief! Thief!

[*Turns to phone, lifts receiver. Holds it a moment, then slams it back into place. Wanders desolately back to the door, opens it and stands staring out into the starless night as the scene dims out. Music: blues—guitar.*]

SCENE FOUR

Late that night. VAL *enters the store, a little unsteadily, with his guitar; goes to the cashbox and rings it open. He counts some bills off a big wad and returns them to the cashbox and the larger wad to the pocket of his snakeskin jacket. Sudden footsteps above; light spills onto stair landing. He quickly moves away from the cashbox as* LADY *appears on the landing in a white sateen robe; she carries a flashlight.*

LADY: Who's that?

[*Music fades out.*]

VAL:—Me.

[*She turns the flashlight on his figure.*]

LADY: Oh, my God, how you scared me!

VAL: You didn't expect me?

LADY: How'd I know it was you I heard come in?

VAL: I thought you give me a room here.

LADY: You left without letting me know if you took it or not. [*She is descending the stairs into store, flashlight still on him.*]

VAL: Catch me turning down something I get for nothing.

LADY: Well, you might have said something so I'd expect you or not.

VAL: I thought you took it for granted.

LADY: I don't take nothing for granted.

[*He starts back to the alcove.*]

Wait!—I'm coming downstairs. . . . [*She descends with the flashlight beam on his face.*]

VAL: You're blinding me with that flashlight.

[*He laughs. She keeps the flashlight on him. He starts back again toward the alcove.*]

LADY: The bed's not made because I didn't expect you.

VAL: That's all right.

LADY: I brought the linen downstairs and you'd cut out.

VAL:—Yeah, well—

[*She picks up linen on counter.*]

Give me that stuff. I can make up my own rack. Tomorrow you'll have to get yourself a new clerk. [*Takes it from her and goes again toward alcove.*] I had a lucky night. [*Exhibits a wad of bills.*]

LADY: *Hey!*

[*He stops near the curtain. She goes and turns on green-shaded bulb over cashbox.*]

—*Did you just open this cashbox?*

VAL:—Why you ask that?

LADY: I thought I heard it ring open a minute ago, that's why I come down here.

VAL:—In your—white satin—kimona?

LADY: *Did you just open the cashbox?!*

VAL:—I wonder who did if I didn't. . . .

LADY: Nobody did if you didn't, but somebody did! [*Opens cashbox and hurriedly counts money. She is trembling violently.*]

VAL: How come you didn't lock the cash up in the safe this evening, Lady?

LADY: Sometimes I forget to.

VAL: That's careless.

LADY:—Why'd you open the cashbox when you come in?

VAL: I opened it twice this evening, once before I went out and again when I come back. I borrowed some money and put it back in the box an' got all this left over! [*Shows her the wad of bills.*] I beat a blackjack dealer five times straight. With this much loot I can retire for the season. . . . [*He returns money to pocket.*]

LADY: *Chicken-feed!*—I'm sorry for you.

VAL: You're sorry for me?

LADY: I'm sorry for you because nobody can help you. I was touched by your—strangeness, your strange talk.—That thing about birds with no feet so they have to sleep on the wind?—I said to myself, "This boy is a bird with no feet so he has to sleep on the wind," and that softened my fool Dago heart and I wanted to help you. . . . Fool, me!—I got what I should of expected. You robbed me while I was upstairs to get sheets to make up your bed!

[*He starts out toward the door.*]

I guess I'm a fool to even feel disappointed.

VAL [*stopping C. and dropping linen on counter*]: You're disappointed in me. I was disappointed in you.

LADY [*coming from behind counter*]:—How did I disappoint you?

VAL: There wasn't no cot behind that curtain before. You put it back there for a purpose.

LADY: It was back there!—folded behind the mirror.

VAL: It wasn't back of no mirror when you told me three times to go and—

LADY [*cutting in*]: I left that money in the cashbox on purpose, to find out if I could trust you.

79

VAL: You got back th' . . .

LADY: No, no, no, I can't trust you, now I know I can't trust you, I got to trust anybody or I don't want him.

VAL: That's OK, I don't expect no character reference from you.

LADY: I'll give you a character reference. I'd say this boy's a peculiar talker! But I wouldn't say a real hard worker or honest. I'd say a peculiar slew-footer that sweet talks you while he's got his hand in the cashbox.

VAL: I took out less than you owed me.

LADY: Don't mix up the issue. I see through you, mister!

VAL: I see through you, Lady.

LADY: What d'you see through me?

VAL: You sure you want me to tell?

LADY: I'd love for you to.

VAL:—A not so young and not so satisfied woman, that hired a man off the highway to do double duty without paying overtime for it. . . . I mean a store clerk days and a stud nights, and—

LADY: God, no! You—! [*She raises her hand as if to strike at him.*] Oh, God no . . . you cheap little—[*Invectives fail her so she uses her fists, hammering at him with them. He seizes her wrists. She struggles a few moments more, then collapses, in chair, sobbing. He lets go of her gently.*]

VAL: It's natural. You felt—lonely. . . .

[*She sobs brokenly against the counter.*]

LADY: Why did you come back here?

VAL: To put back the money I took so you wouldn't re-member me as not honest or grateful—[*He picks up his guitar and starts to the door nodding gravely. She catches her breath; rushes to intercept him, spreading her arms like a crossbar over the door.*]

LADY: NO, NO, DON'T GO . . . I NEED YOU!!!

[He faces her for five beats. The true passion of her outcry touches him then, and he turns about and crosses to the alcove. . . . As he draws the curtain across it he looks back at her.]

TO LIVE. . . . TO GO ON LIVING!!!

[Music fades in—"Lady's Love Song"—guitar. He closes the curtain and turns on the light behind it, making it translucent. Through an opening in the alcove entrance, we see him sitting down with his guitar. LADY *picks up the linen and crosses to the alcove like a spellbound child. Just outside it she stops, frozen with uncertainty, a conflict of feelings, but then he begins to whisper the words of a song so tenderly that she is able to draw the curtain open and enter the alcove. He looks up gravely at her from his guitar. She closes the curtain behind her. Its bizarre design, a gold tree with white birds and scarlet fruit in it, is softly translucent with the bulb lighted behind it. The guitar continues softly for a few moments; stops; the stage darkens till only the curtain of the alcove is clearly visible.]*

CURTAIN

ACT THREE

An early morning. The Saturday before Easter. The sleeping alcove is lighted. VAL *is smoking, half dressed, on the edge of the cot.* LADY *comes running, panting downstairs, her hair loose, in dressing robe and slippers and calls out in a panicky, shrill whisper.*

LADY: Val! Val, he's comin' downstairs!

VAL [*hoarse with sleep*]: Who's—what?

LADY: Jabe!

VAL: Jabe?

LADY: I swear he is, he's coming downstairs!

VAL: What of it?

LADY: Jesus, will you get up and put some clothes on? The damned nurse told him that he could come down in the store to check over the stock! You want him to catch you half dressed on that bed there?

VAL: Don't he know I sleep here?

LADY: Nobody knows you sleep here but you and me.

[*Voices above.*]

Oh, God!—they've started.

NURSE: Don't hurry now. Take one step at a time.

[*Footsteps on stairs, slow, shuffling. The professional, nasal cheer of a nurse's voice.*]

LADY [*panicky*]: Get your shirt on! Come out!

NURSE: That's right. One step at a time, one step at a time, lean on my shoulder and take one step at a time.

82

[VAL *rises, still dazed from sleep.* LADY *gasps and sweeps the curtain across the alcove just a moment before the descending figures enter the sight-lines on the landing.* LADY *breathes like an exhausted runner as she backs away from the alcove and assumes a forced smile.* JABE *and the nurse,* MISS PORTER, *appear on the landing of the stairs and at the same moment scudding clouds expose the sun. A narrow window on the landing admits a brilliant shaft of light upon the pair. They have a bizarre and awful appearance, the tall man, his rusty black suit hanging on him like an empty sack, his eyes burning malignantly from his yellow face, leaning on a stumpy little woman with bright pink or orange hair, clad all in starched white, with a voice that purrs with the faintly contemptuous cheer and sweetness of those hired to care for the dying.*]

NURSE: Aw, now, just look at that, that nice bright sun comin' out.

LADY: Miss Porter? It's—it's cold down here!

JABE: What's she say?

NURSE: She says it's cold down here.

LADY: The—the—the air's not warm enough yet, the air's not heated!

NURSE: He's determined to come right down, Mrs. Torrance.

LADY: I know but—

NURSE: Wild horses couldn't hold him a minute longer.

JABE [*exhausted*]:—Let's—rest here a minute. . . .

LADY [*eagerly*]: Yes! Rest there a minute!

NURSE: Okay. We'll rest here a minute. . . .

[*They sit down side by side on a bench under the artificial palm tree in the shaft of light.* JABE *glares into the light*

83

like a fierce dying old beast. There are sounds from the alcove. To cover them up, LADY *keeps making startled, laughing sounds in her throat, half laughing, half panting, chafing her hands together at the foot of the stairs, and coughing falsely.*]

JABE: Lady, what's wrong? Why are you so excited?

LADY: It seems like a miracle to me.

JABE: What seems like a miracle to you?

LADY: You coming downstairs.

JABE: You never thought I would come downstairs again?

LADY: Not this quick! Not as quick as this, Jabe! Did you think he would pick up as quick as this, Miss Porter?

[JABE *rises.*]

NURSE: Ready?

JABE: Ready.

NURSE: He's doing fine, knock wood.

LADY: Yes, knock wood, knock wood!

[*Drums counter loudly with her knuckles.* VAL *steps silently from behind the alcove curtain as the* NURSE *and* JABE *resume their slow, shuffling descent of the stairs.*]

[*Moving back to D.R.C.*] You got to be careful not to overdo. You don't want another setback. Ain't that right, Miss Porter?

NURSE: Well, it's my policy to mobilize the patient.

LADY [*to* VAL *in a shrill whisper*]: Coffee's boiling, take the Goddamn coffee pot off the burner! [*She gives* VAL *a panicky signal to go in the alcove.*]

JABE: Who're you talking to, Lady?

LADY: To—to—to Val, the clerk! I told him to—get you a—chair!

JABE: Who's that?

LADY: Val, Val, the clerk, you know Val!

JABE: Not yet. I'm anxious to meet him. Where is he?

LADY: Right here, right here, here's Val!

[VAL *returns from the alcove.*]

JABE: He's here bright and early.

LADY: The early bird catches the worm!

JABE: That's right. Where is the worm?

LADY [*loudly*]: Ha ha!

NURSE: Careful! One step at a time, Mr. Torrance.

LADY: Saturday before Easter's our biggest sales-day of the year, I mean second biggest, but sometimes it's even bigger than Christmas Eve! So I told Val to get here a half hour early.

[JABE *misses his step and stumbles to foot of stairs.* LADY *screams.* NURSE *rushes down to him.* VAL *advances and raises the man to his feet.*]

VAL: Here. Here.

LADY: Oh, my God.

NURSE: Oh, oh!

JABE: I'm all right.

NURSE: Are you sure?

LADY: Are you sure?

JABE: Let me go! [*He staggers to lean against counter, panting, glaring, with a malignant smile.*]

LADY: Oh, my God. Oh, my—God. . . .

JABE: This is the boy that works here?

LADY: Yes, this is the clerk I hired to help us out, Jabe.

JABE: How is he doing?

LADY: Fine, fine.

JABE: He's mighty good-looking. Do women give him much trouble?

LADY: When school lets out the high-school girls are thick as flies in this store!

JABE: How about older women? Don't he attract older women? The older ones are the buyers, they got the money. They sweat it out of their husbands and throw it away! What's your salary, boy, how much do I pay you?

LADY: Twenty-two fifty a week.

JABE: You're getting him cheap.

VAL: I get—commissions.

JABE: Commissions?

VAL: Yes. One percent of all sales.

JABE: Oh? Oh? I didn't know about that.

LADY: I knew he would bring in trade and he brings it in.

JABE: I bet.

LADY: Val, get Jabe a chair, he ought to sit down.

JABE: No, I don't want to sit down. I want to take a look at the new confectionery.

LADY: Oh, yes, yes! Take a look at it! Val, Val, turn on the lights in the confectionery! I want Jabe to see the way I done it over! I'm—real—*proud!*

[VAL *crosses and switches on light in confectionery. The bulbs in the arches and the juke box light up.*]

Go in and look at it, Jabe. I am real proud of it!

[*He stares at* LADY *a moment; then shuffles slowly into the spectral radiance of the confectionery.* LADY *moves D.C. At the same time a calliope becomes faintly audible and slowly but steadily builds.* MISS PORTER *goes with the patient, holding his elbow.*]

VAL [*returning to* LADY]: He looks like death.

LADY [*moving away from him*]: *Hush!*

[VAL *goes up above counter and stands in the shadows.*]

NURSE: Well, isn't this artistic.

JABE: Yeh. Artistic as hell.

NURSE: I never seen anything like it before.

JABE: Nobody else did either.

NURSE [*coming back to U.R.C.*]: Who done these decorations?

LADY [*defiantly*]: I did them, all by myself!

NURSE: What do you know. It sure is something artistic.

[*Calliope is now up loud.*]

JABE [*coming back to D.R.*]: Is there a circus or carnival in the county?

LADY: What?

JABE: That sounds like a circus calliope on the highway.

LADY: That's no circus calliope. It's advertising the gala opening of the Torrance Confectionery tonight!

JABE: Doing what did you say?

LADY: It's announcing the opening of our confectionery, it's going all over Glorious Hill this morning and all over Sunset and Lyon this afternoon. Hurry on here so you can

87

see it go by the store. [*She rushes excitedly to open the front door as the ragtime music of the calliope approaches.*]

JABE: I married a live one, Miss Porter. How much does that damn thing cost me?

LADY: You'll be surprised how little. [*She is talking with an hysterical vivacity now.*] I hired it for a song!

JABE: How much of a song did you hire it for?

LADY [*closing door*]: Next to nothing, seven-fifty an hour! And it covers three towns in Two River County!

[*Calliope fades out.*]

JABE [*with a muted ferocity*]: Miss Porter, I married a live one! Didn't I marry a live one? [*Switches off lights in confectionery*] Her daddy "The Wop" was just as much of a live one till he burned up.

[LADY *gasps as if struck.*]

[*With a slow, ugly grin:*] He had a wine garden on the north shore of Moon Lake. The new confectionery sort of reminds me of it. But he made a mistake, he made a bad mistake, one time, selling liquor to niggers. We burned him out. We burned him out, house and orchard and vines and "The Wop" was burned up trying to fight the fire. [*He turns.*] I think I better go up.

LADY:—Did you say "WE"?

JABE:—I have a kind of a cramp. . . .

NURSE [*taking his arm*]: Well, let's go up.

JABE:—Yes, I better go up. . . .

[*They cross to stairs. Calliope fades in.*]

LADY [*almost shouting as she moves D.C.*]: Jabe, did you say "WE" did it, did you say "WE" did it?

JABE [*at foot of stairs, stops, turns*]: Yes, I said *"We"* did it. You heard me, Lady.

NURSE: One step at a time, one step at a time, take it easy.

[*They ascend gradually to the landing and above. The calliope passes directly before the store and a clown is seen, or heard, shouting through megaphone.*]

CLOWN: Don't forget tonight, folks, the gala opening of the Torrance Confectionery, free drinks and free favors, don't forget it, the gala opening of the confectionery.

[*Fade.* JABE *and the* NURSE *disappear above the landing. Calliope gradually fades. A hoarse cry above. The* NURSE *runs back downstairs, exclaiming:*]

NURSE: He's bleeding, he's having a hemm'rhage! [*Runs to phone.*] Dr. Buchanan's office! [*Turns again to* LADY.] Your husband is having a hemm'rhage!

[*Calliope is loud still.* LADY *appears not to hear. She speaks to* VAL:]

LADY: Did you hear what he said? He said "We" did it, "WE" burned—house—vines—orchard—"The Wop" burned fighting the fire. . . .

[*The scene dims out; calliope fades out.*]

SCENE TWO

Sunset of the same day. At rise VAL *is alone. He is standing stock-still down center stage, almost beneath the proscenium, in the tense, frozen attitude of a wild animal listening to something that warns it of danger, his head turned as if he were looking off stage left, out over the house, frowning slightly, attentively. After a moment he mutters something sharply, and his body relaxes; he takes out a cigarette and crosses to the store entrance, opens the door and stands looking out. It has been raining steadily and will rain again in a while, but right now it is clearing: the sun breaks through, suddenly, with great brilliance; and almost at the same instant, at some distance, a woman cries out a great hoarse cry of terror and exaltation; the cry is repeated as she comes running nearer.*

VEE TALBOTT *appears through the window as if blind and demented, stiff, groping gestures, shielding her eyes with one arm as she feels along the store window for the entrance, gasping for breath.* VAL *steps aside, taking hold of her arm to guide her into the store. For a few moments she leans weakly, blindly panting for breath against the oval glass of the door, then calls out.*

VEE: I'm—*struck blind!*

VAL: You can't see?

VEE:—No! Nothing....

VAL [*assisting her to stool below counter*]: Set down here, Mrs. Talbott.

VEE:—Where?

VAL [*pushing her gently*]: Here.

[VEE *sinks moaning onto stool.*]

What hurt your eyes, Mrs. Talbott, what happened to your eyes?

90

VEE [*drawing a long, deep breath*]: The vision I waited and prayed for all my life long!

VAL: You had a vision?

VEE: I saw the eyes of my Saviour!—They struck me blind. [*Leans forward, clasping her eyes in anguish.*] Ohhhh, they burned out my eyes!

VAL: Lean back.

VEE: Eyeballs burn like fire. . . .

VAL [*going off R.*]: I'll get you something cold to put on your eyes.

VEE: I knew a vision was coming, oh, I had many signs!

VAL [*in confectionery*]: It must be a terrible shock to have a vision. . . . [*He speaks gravely, gently, scooping chipped ice from the soft-drink cooler and wrapping it in his handkerchief.*]

VEE [*with the naïveté of a child, as* VAL *comes back to her*]: I *thought* I would see my Saviour on the day of His passion, which was yesterday, Good Friday, that's when I expected to see Him. But I was mistaken, I was—disappointed. Yesterday passed and nothing, nothing much happened but—today—

[VAL *places handkerchief over her eyes.*]

—this afternoon, somehow I pulled myself together and walked outdoors and started to go to pray in the empty church and meditate on the Rising of Christ tomorrow. Along the road as I walked, thinking about the mysteries of Easter, veils!

—[*She makes a long shuddering word out of "veils."*]—

seemed to drop off my eyes! Light, oh, light! I never have seen such brilliance! It *PRICKED* my eyeballs like *NEEDLES!*

VAL:—Light?

91

VEE: Yes, yes, light. YOU know, you know we live in light and shadow, that's, that's what we *live* in, a world of—*light* and—*shadow....*

VAL: Yes. In light and shadow. [*He nods with complete understanding and agreement. They are like two children who have found life's meaning, simply and quietly, along a country road.*]

VEE: A world of light and shadow is what we live in, and —it's—confusing....

[*A man is peering in at store window.*]

VAL: Yeah, they—*do* get—*mixed....*

VEE: Well, and then—[*Hesitates to recapture her vision.*] —I heard this clap of thunder! Sky!—Split open!—And there in the split-open sky, I saw, I tell you, I *saw* the TWO HUGE BLAZING EYES OF JESUS CHRIST RISEN!—Not crucified but Risen! I mean Crucified and *then* RISEN!—The blazing eyes of Christ Risen! And then a great—[*Raises both arms and makes a great sweeping motion to describe an apocalyptic disturbance of the atmosphere.*]—His hand!—Invisible! —I didn't *see* his hand!—But it *touched* me—*here!* [*She seizes* VAL'S *hand and presses it to her great heaving bosom.*]

TALBOTT [*appearing R. in confectionery, furiously*]: VEE!

[*She starts up, throwing the compress from her eyes. Utters a sharp gasp and staggers backward with terror and blasted ecstacy and dismay and belief, all confused in her look.*]

VEE: You!

TALBOTT: VEE!

VEE: *You!*

TALBOTT [*advancing*]: VEE!

VEE [*making two syllables of the word "eyes"*]:—The Ey —es! [*She collapses, forward, falls to her knees, her arms*

92

thrown about VAL. *He seizes her to lift her. Two or three men are peering in at the store window.*]

TALBOTT [*pushing* VAL *away*]: Let go of her, don't put your hands on my wife! [*He seizes her roughly and hauls her to the door.* VAL *moves up to help* VEE.] Don't move. [*At door, to* VAL:] I'm coming back.

VAL: I'm not goin' nowhere.

TALBOTT [*to* DOG, *as he goes off L. with* VEE]: Dog, go in there with that boy.

VOICE [*outside*]: Sheriff caught him messin' with his wife.

[*Repeat:* ANOTHER VOICE *at a distance.* "DOG" HAMMA *enters and stands silently beside the door while there is a continued murmur of excited voices on the street. The following scene should be underplayed, played almost casually, like the performance of some familiar ritual.*]

VAL: What do you want?

[DOG *says nothing but removes from his pocket and opens a spring-blade knife and moves to D.R.* PEE WEE *enters. Through the open door—voices.*]

VOICES [*outside*]:—Son of a low-down bitch foolin' with—

—That's right, ought to be—

—Cut the son of a—

VAL: What do you—?

[PEE WEE *closes the door and silently stands beside it, opening a spring-blade knife.* VAL *looks from one to the other.*]

—It's six o'clock. Store's closed.

[*Men chuckle like dry leaves rattling.* VAL *crosses toward the door; is confronted by* TALBOTT; *stops short.*]

TALBOTT: Boy, I said stay here.

93

VAL: I'm not—goin' nowhere. . . .

TALBOTT: Stand back under that light.

VAL: Which light?

TALBOTT: That light.

[*Points.* VAL *goes behind counter.*]

I want to look at you while I run through some photos of men wanted.

VAL: I'm not wanted.

TALBOTT: A good-looking boy like you is always wanted.

[*Men chuckle.* VAL *stands in hot light under green-shaded bulb.* TALBOTT *shuffles through photos he has removed from his pocket.*]

—How tall are you, boy?

VAL: Never measured.

TALBOTT: How much do you weigh?

VAL: Never weighed.

TALBOTT: Got any scars or marks of identification on your face or body?

VAL: No, sir.

TALBOTT: Open your shirt.

VAL: What for? [*He doesn't.*]

TALBOTT: Open his shirt for him, Dog.

[DOG *steps quickly forward and rips shirt open to waist.* VAL *starts forward; men point knives; he draws back.*]

That's right, stay there, boy. What did you do before?

[PEE WEE *sits on stairs.*]

VAL: Before—what?

TALBOTT: Before you come here?

VAL:—Traveled and—played. . . .

TALBOTT: Played?

DOG [*advancing to C.*]: What?

PEE WEE: With wimmen?

[DOG *laughs.*]

VAL: No. Played guitar—and sang. . . .

[VAL *touches guitar on counter.*]

TALBOTT: Let me see that guitar.

VAL: Look at it. But don't touch it. I don't let nobody but musicians touch it.

[*Men come close.*]

DOG: What're you smiling for, boy?

PEE WEE: He ain't smiling, his mouth's just twitching like a dead chicken's foot.

[*They laugh.*]

TALBOTT: What is all that writing on the guitar?

VAL:—Names. . . .

TALBOTT: What of?

VAL: Autographs of musicians dead and living.

[*Men read aloud the names printed on the guitar: Bessie Smith, Leadbelly, Woody Guthrie, Jelly Roll Morton, etc. They bend close to it, keeping the open knife blades pointed at* VAL'S *body;* DOG *touches neck of the guitar, draws it toward him.* VAL *suddenly springs, with catlike agility, onto the counter. He runs along it, kicking at their hands as they catch at his legs. The* NURSE *runs down to the landing.*]

MISS PORTER: *What's going on?*

95

TALBOTT [*at the same time*]: *Stop that!*

[JABE *calls hoarsely above.*]

MISS PORTER [*excitedly, all in one breath, as* JABE *calls*]: Where's Mrs. Torrance? I got a very sick man up there and his wife's disappeared.

[JABE *calls out again.*]

I been on a whole lot of cases but never seen one where a wife showed no concern for a—

[JABE *cries out again. Her voice fades out as she returns above.*]

TALBOTT [*overlapping* NURSE'S *speech*]: Dog! Pee Wee! You all stand back from that counter. Dog, why don't you an' Pee Wee go up an' see Jabe. Leave me straighten this boy out, go on, go on up.

PEE WEE: C'mon, Dawg. . . .

[*They go up.* VAL *remains panting on counter.*]

TALBOTT [*sits in shoe chair at R. window. In* TALBOTT'S *manner there is a curious, half-abashed gentleness, when alone with the boy, as if he recognized the purity in him and was, truly, for the moment, ashamed of the sadism implicit in the occurrence*]: Awright, boy. Git on down off th' counter, I ain't gonna touch y'r guitar.

[VAL *jumps off counter.*]

But I'm gonna tell you something. They's a certain county I know of which has a big sign at the county line that says, "Nigger, don't let the sun go down on you in this county." That's all it says, it don't threaten nothing, it just says, "Nigger, don't let the sun go down on you in this county!" [*Chuckles hoarsely. Rises and takes a step toward* VAL.]

Well, son! You ain't a nigger and this is not that county, but, son, I want you to just imagine that you seen a sign that said to you: "Boy, don't let the sun rise on you in this county." I said "rise," not "go down" because it's too close to sunset for you to git packed an' move on before that. But I think if you value that instrument in your hands as much as you seem to, you'll simplify my job by not allowing the sun tomorrow to rise on you in this county. 'S that understood, now, boy?

[VAL *stares at him, expressionless, panting.*]

[*Crossing to door*] I *hope* so. I don't like *violence.* [*He looks back and nods at* VAL *from the door. Then goes outside in the fiery afterglow of the sunset. Dogs bark in the distance. Music fades in: "Dog Howl Blues"—minor—guitar. Pause in which* VAL *remains motionless, cradling guitar in his arms. Then* VAL'S *faraway, troubled look is resolved in a slight, abrupt nod of his head. He sweeps back the alcove curtain and enters the alcove and closes the curtain behind him. Lights dim down to indicate a division of scenes.*]

Half an hour later. The lighting is less realistic than in the previous scenes of the play. The interior of the store is so dim that only the vertical lines of the pillars and such selected items as the palm tree on the stair landing and the ghostly paper vineyard of the confectionery are plainly visible. The view through the great front window has virtually become the background of the action: A singing wind sweeps clouds before the moon so that the witchlike country brightens and dims and brightens again. The Marshall's hounds are restless: their baying is heard now and then. A lamp outside the door sometimes catches a figure that moves past with mysterious urgency, calling out softly and raising an arm to beckon, like a shade in the under kingdom.

At rise, or when the stage is lighted again, it is empty but footsteps are descending the stairs as DOLLY *and* BEULAH *rush into the store and call out, in soft shouts:*

DOLLY: Dawg?

BEULAH: Pee Wee?

EVA TEMPLE [*appearing on landing and calling down softly in the superior tone of a privileged attendant in a sick-chamber*]: Please don't shout!—Mr. Binnings and Mr. Hamma [*Names of the two husbands*] are upstairs sitting with Jabe. . . . [*She continues her descent. Then* EVA TEMPLE *appears, sobbing, on landing.*]

—Come down carefully, Sister.

SISTER: Help me, I'm all to pieces. . . .

[EVA *ignores this request and faces the two women.*]

BEULAH: Has the bleedin' quit yit?

EVA: The hemorrhage seems to have stopped. Sister, Sister, pull yourself together, we all have to face these things sometime in life.

DOLLY: Has he sunk into a coma?

EVA: No. Cousin Jabe is conscious. Nurse Porter says his pulse is remarkably strong for a man that lost so much blood. Of course he's had a transfusion.

SISTER: Two of 'em.

EVA [*crossing to* DOLLY]: Yais, an' they put him on glucose. His strength came back like magic.

BEULAH: She up there?

EVA: *Who?*

BEULAH: Lady!

EVA: No! When last reported she had just stepped into the Glorious Hill Beauty Parlor.

BEULAH: You don't mean it.

EVA: Ask Sister!

SISTER: She's planning to go ahead with—! *81128*

EVA:—The gala opening of the confectionery. Switch on the lights in there, Sister.

[SISTER *crosses and switches on lights and moves off R. The decorated confectionery is lighted.* DOLLY *and* BEULAH *exclaim in awed voices.*]

—Of course it's not normal behavior; it's downright lunacy, but still that's no excuse for it! And when she called up at five, about one hour ago, it wasn't to ask about Jabe, oh, no, she didn't mention his name. She asked if Ruby Lightfoot had delivered a case of Seagram's. Yais, she just shouted that question and hung up the phone, before I could—[*She crosses and goes off R.*]

99

BEULAH [*going into confectionery*]: *Oh, I understand, now! Now I see what she's up to!* Electric moon, cut-out silver-paper stars and artificial vines? Why, it's her father's wine garden on Moon Lake she's turned this room into!

DOLLY [*suddenly as she sits in shoe chair*]: Here she comes, here she comes!

[*The* TEMPLE SISTERS *retreat from view in confectionery as* LADY *enters the store. She wears a hooded rain-cape and carries a large paper shopping bag and paper carton box.*]

LADY: Go on, ladies, don't stop, my ears are burning!

BEULAH [*coming in to U.R.C.*]:—Lady, oh, Lady, Lady. . . .

LADY: Why d'you speak my name in that pitiful voice? Hanh? [*Throws back hood of cape, her eyes blazing, and places bag and box on counter.*] *Val? Val!* Where is that boy that works here?

[DOLLY *shakes her head.*]

I guess he's havin' a T-bone steak with French fries and coleslaw fo' ninety-five cents at the Blue Bird. . . .

[*Sounds in confectionery.*]

Who's in the confectionery, is that you, Val?

[TEMPLE SISTERS *emerge and stalk past her.*]

Going, girls?

[*They go out of store.*]

Yes, gone! [*She laughs and throws off rain-cape, onto counter, revealing a low-cut gown, triple strand of pearls and a purple satin-ribboned corsage.*]

BEULAH [*sadly*]: How long have I known you, Lady?

LADY [*going behind counter, unpacks paper hats and whistles*]: A long time, Beulah. I think you remember when

100

my people come here on a banana boat from Palermo, Sicily, by way of Caracas, Venezuela, yes, with a grind-organ and a monkey my papa had bought in Venezuela. I was not much bigger than the monkey, ha ha! You remember the monkey? The man that sold Papa the monkey said it was a very young monkey, but he was a liar, it was a very old monkey, it was on its last legs, ha ha ha! But it was a well-dressed monkey. *[Coming around to R. of counter]* It had a green velvet suit and a little red cap that it tipped and a tambourine that it passed around for money, ha ha ha. . . . The grind-organ played and the monkey danced in the sun, ha ha!—*"O Sole Mio, Da Da Da daaa . . . !"* *[Sits in chair at counter]*—One day, the monkey danced too much in the sun and it was a very old monkey and it dropped dead. . . . My Papa, he turned to the people, he made them a bow and he said, "The show is over, the monkey is dead." Ha ha!

[Slight pause. Then DOLLY *pipes up venomously:]*

DOLLY: Ain't it wonderful Lady can be so brave?

BEULAH: Yaiss, wonderful! Hanh. . . .

LADY: For me the show is not over, the monkey is not dead yet! *[Then suddenly:]* Val, is that you, Val?

[Someone has entered the confectionery door, out of sight, and the draught of air has set the wind-chimes tinkling wildly. LADY *rushes forward but stops short as* CAROL *appears. She wears a trench coat and a white sailor's cap with a turned-down brim, inscribed with the name of a vessel and a date, past or future, memory or anticipation.]*

DOLLY: Well, here's your first customer, Lady.

LADY *[going behind counter]*:—Carol, that room ain't open.

CAROL: There's a big sign outside that says "Open Tonite!"

LADY: It ain't open to you.

CAROL: I have to stay here a while. They stopped my car, you see, I don't have a license; my license has been revoked and I have to find someone to drive me across the river.

LADY: You can call a taxi.

CAROL: I heard that the boy that works for you is leaving tonight and I—

LADY: *Who said he's leaving?*

CAROL [*crossing to counter*]: Sheriff Talbott. The County Marshall suggested I get him to drive me over the river since he'd be crossing it too.

LADY: You got some mighty wrong information!

CAROL: Where is he? I don't see him?

LADY: Why d'you keep coming back here bothering that boy? He's not interested in you! Why would he be leaving here tonight?

[*Door opens off as she comes from behind counter.*]

Val, is that you, Val?

[CONJURE MAN *enters through confectionery, mumbling rapidly, holding out something.* BEULAH *and* DOLLY *take flight out the door with cries of revulsion.*]

No conjure stuff, go away!

[*He starts to withdraw.*]

CAROL [*crossing to U.R.C.*]: Uncle! The Choctaw cry! I'll give you a dollar for it.

[LADY *turns away with a gasp, with a gesture of refusal. The* NEGRO *nods, then throws back his turkey neck and utters a series of sharp barking sounds that rise to a sustained cry of great intensity and wildness. The cry produces*

102

a violent reaction in the building. BEULAH *and* DOLLY *run out of the store.* LADY *does not move but she catches her breath.* DOG *and* PEE WEE *run down the stairs with ad libs and hustle the* NEGRO *out of the store, ignoring* LADY, *as their wives call:* "PEE WEE!" *and* "DAWG!" *outside on the walk.* VAL *sweeps back the alcove curtain and appears as if the cry were his cue. Above, in the sick room, hoarse, outraged shouts that subside with exhaustion.* CAROL *crosses downstage and speaks to the audience and to herself:*]

CAROL: Something is still wild in the country! This country used to be wild, the men and women were wild and there was a wild sort of sweetness in their hearts, for each other, but now it's sick with neon, it's broken out sick, with neon, like most other places. . . . I'll wait outside in my car. It's the fastest thing on wheels in Two River County!

[*She goes out of the store R.* LADY *stares at* VAL *with great asking eyes, a hand to her throat.*]

LADY [*with false boldness*]: Well, ain't you going with her?

VAL: I'm going with no one I didn't come here with. And I come here with no one.

LADY: Then get into your white jacket. I need your services in that room there tonight.

[VAL *regards her steadily for several beats.*]

[*Clapping her hands together twice*] Move, move, stop goofing! The Delta Brilliant lets out in half'n hour and they'll be driving up here. You got to shave ice for the setups!

VAL [*as if he thought she'd gone crazy*]: "Shave ice for the setups"? [*He moves up to counter.*]

LADY: Yes, an' call Ruby Lightfoot, tell her I need me a dozen more half-pints of Seagram's. They all call for Seven-

103

and-Sevens. You know how t' sell bottle goods under a counter? It's OK. We're gonna git paid for protection. [*Gasps, touching her diaphragm*] But one thing you gotta watch out for is sellin' to minors. Don't serve liquor to minors. Ask for his driver's license if they's any doubt. Anybody born earlier than—let's see, twenty-one from—oh, I'll figure it later. Hey! Move! Move! Stop goofing!

VAL [*placing guitar on counter*]:—You're the one that's goofing, not me, Lady.

LADY: Move, I said, *move!*

VAL: What kick are you on, are you on a benny kick, Lady? 'Ve you washed down a couple of bennies with a pot of black coffee t' make you come on strong for th' three o'clock show? [*His mockery is gentle, almost tender, but he has already made a departure; he is back in the all-night bars with the B-girls and raffish entertainers. He stands at counter as she rushes about. As she crosses between the two rooms, he reaches out to catch hold of her bare arm and he pulls her to him and grips her arms.*]

LADY: Hey!

VAL: Will you quit thrashin' around like a hooked catfish?

LADY: Go git in y'r white jacket an'—

VAL: Sit down. I want to talk to you.

LADY: I don't have time.

VAL: I got to reason with you.

LADY: It's not possible to.

VAL: You can't open a night-place here this night.

LADY: You bet your sweet life I'm *going* to!

VAL: Not *me*, not *my* sweet life!

LADY: I'm betting *my* life on it! Sweet or *not* sweet, I'm—

104

VAL: Yours is yours, mine is mine. . . . [*He releases her with a sad shrug.*]

LADY: You don't get the point, huh? There's a man up there that set fire to my father's wine garden and I lost my life in it, yeah, I lost my life in it, *three* lives was lost in it, two *born* lives and one—*not*. . . . I was made to commit a *murder* by him up there! [*Has frozen momentarily*]—I want that man to see the wine garden come open again when he's dying! I want him to hear it coming open again here tonight! While he's dying. It's necessary, no power on earth can stop it. Hell, I don't even want it, it's just necessary, it's just something's got to be done to square things away, to, to, to—be *not defeated! You get me? Just to be not defeated!* Ah, oh, I won't be defeated, not again, in my life! [*Embraces him*] Thank you for staying here with me!—God bless you for it. . . . Now please go and get in your white jacket . . .

[*VAL looks at her as if he were trying to decide between a natural sensibility of heart and what his life's taught him since he left Witches' Bayou. Then he sighs again, with the same slight, sad shrug, and crosses into alcove to put on a jacket and remove from under his cot a canvas-wrapped package of his belongings. LADY takes paper hats and carnival stuff from counter, crosses into confectionery and puts them on the tables, then starts back but stops short as she sees VAL come out of alcove with his snakeskin jacket and luggage.*]

LADY: That's not your white jacket, that's that snakeskin jacket you had on when you come here.

VAL: I come and I go in this jacket.

LADY: *Go,* did you say?

VAL: Yes, ma'am, I did, I said go. All that stays to be settled is a little matter of wages.

105

[*The dreaded thing's happened to her. This is what they call "the moment of truth" in the bull ring, when the matador goes in over the horns of the bull to plant the mortal sword-thrust.*]

LADY:—So you're—cutting out, are you?

VAL: My gear's all packed. I'm catchin' the southbound bus.

LADY: Uh-huh, in a pig's eye. You're not conning me, mister. She's waiting for you outside in her high-powered car and you're—

[*Sudden footsteps on stairs. They break apart,* VAL *puts suitcase down, drawing back into shadow, as* NURSE PORTER *appears on the stair landing.*]

NURSE PORTER: Miss Torrance, are you down there?

LADY [*crossing to foot of stairs*]: Yeah. I'm here. I'm back.

NURSE PORTER: Can I talk to you up here about Mr. Torrance?

LADY [*shouting to* NURSE]: I'll be up in a minute.

[*Door closes above.* LADY *turns to* VAL:] OK, now, mister. You're scared about something, ain't you?

VAL: I been threatened with violence if I stay here.

LADY: I got paid for protection in this county, plenty paid for it, and it covers you too.

VAL: No, ma'am. My time is up here.

LADY: Y' say that like you'd served a sentence in jail.

VAL: I got in deeper than I meant to, Lady.

LADY: Yeah, and how about me?

VAL [*going to her*]: I would of cut out before you got back to the store, but I wanted to tell you something I never told no one before. [*Places hand on her shoulder.*] I feel a true love for you, Lady! [*He kisses her.*] I'll wait for you out of this county, just name the time and the . . .

LADY [*moving back*]: Oh, don't talk about love, not to me. It's easy to say "Love, Love!" with fast and free transportation waiting right out the door for you!

VAL: D'you remember some things I told you about me the night we met here?

LADY [*crossing to R.C.*]: Yeah, many things. Yeah, temperature of a dog. And some bird, oh, yeah, without legs so it had to sleep on the wind!

VAL [*through her speech*]: Naw, not that; not that.

LADY: And how you could burn down a woman? I said "Bull!" I take that back. You can! You can burn down a woman and stamp on her ashes to make sure the fire is put out!

VAL: I mean what I said about gettin' away from . . .

LADY: How long've you held this first steady job in your life?

VAL: Too long, too long!

LADY: Four months and five days, mister. All right! How much pay have you took?

VAL: I told you to keep out all but—

LADY: Y'r living expenses. I can give you the figures to a dime. Eighty-five bucks, no, ninety! Chicken-feed, mister! Y'know how much you got coming? IF you get it? I don't need paper to figure, I got it all in my head. You got five hundred and eighty-six bucks coming to you, not, not chicken-feed, that. But, mister. [*Gasps for breath*]—If you try to walk out on me, now, tonight, without notice!—You're going to get just nothing! A great big zero. . . .

107

[*Somebody hollers at door off R.: "Hey! You open?" She rushes toward it shouting, "CLOSED! CLOSED! GO AWAY!"*—VAL *crosses to the cashbox. She turns back toward him, gasps:*]

Now you watch your next move and I'll watch mine. You open that cashbox and I swear I'll throw open that door and holler, clerk's robbing the store!

VAL:—Lady?

LADY [*fiercely*]: Hanh?

VAL:—Nothing, you've—

LADY:—Hanh?

VAL: Blown your stack. I will go without pay.

LADY [*coming to C.*]: Then you ain't understood me! With or without pay, you're staying!

VAL: I've got my gear. [*Picks up suitcase. She rushes to seize his guitar.*]

LADY: Then I'll go up and git mine! And take this with me, just t'make sure you wait till I'm—[*She moves back to R.C. He puts suitcase down.*]

VAL [*advancing toward her*]: Lady, what're you—?

LADY [*entreating with guitar raised*]: *Don't—!*

VAL:—Doing with—

LADY:—*Don't!*

VAL:—my guitar!

LADY: *Holding it for security while I—*

VAL: Lady, you been a lunatic since this morning!

LADY: Longer, longer than morning! I'm going to keep hold of your "life companion" while I pack! I am! I am goin' to pack an' go, if you go, where you go!

[*He makes a move toward her. She crosses below and around to counter.*]

You didn't think so, you actually didn't think so? What was I going to do, in your opinion? What, in your opinion, would I be doing? Stay on here in a store full of bottles and boxes while you go far, while you go fast and far, without me having your—forwarding address!—even?

VAL: I'll—give you a forwarding address. . . .

LADY: Thanks, oh, thanks! Would I take your forwarding address back of that curtain? "Oh, dear forwarding address, hold me, kiss me, be faithful!" [*Utters grotesque, stifled cry; presses fist to mouth.*]

[*He advances cautiously, hand stretched toward the guitar. She retreats above to U.R.C., biting lip, eyes flaring. JABE knocks above.*]

Stay back! You want me to smash it!

VAL [*D.C.*]: He's—knocking for you. . . .

LADY: I know! Death's knocking for me! Don't you think I hear him, knock, knock, knock? It sounds like what it is! Bones knocking bones. . . . Ask me how it felt to be coupled with death up there, and I can tell you. My skin crawled when he touched me. But I endured it. I guess my heart knew that somebody must be coming to take me out of this hell! You did. You came. Now look at me! I'm alive once more! [*Convulsive sobbing controlled: continues more calmly and harshly:*]

—*I won't wither in dark!* Got that through your skull? Now. Listen! Everything in this rotten store is yours, not just your pay, but everything Death's scraped together down here! —but Death has got to die before we can go. . . . You got that memorized, now?—Then get into your white jacket!—

109

*Tonight is the gala opening—[Rushes through confectionery.]
—of the confectionery—*

[VAL *runs and seizes her arm holding guitar. She breaks
violently free.*]

*Smash me against a rock and I'll smash your guitar! I will,
if you—*

[*Rapid footsteps on stairs.*]

Oh, Miss Porter!

[*She motions* VAL *back. He retreats into alcove.* LADY *puts
guitar down beside juke-box.* MISS PORTER *is descending
the stairs.*]

NURSE PORTER [*descending watchfully*]: You been out a
long time.

LADY [*moving U.R.C.*]: Yeah, well, I had lots of—[*Her
voice expires breathlessly. She stares fiercely, blindly, into the
other's hard face.*]

NURSE PORTER:—Of what?

LADY: Things to—things to—take care of. . . . [*Draws a
deep, shuddering breath, clenched fist to her bosom.*]

NURSE PORTER: Didn't I hear you shouting to someone
just now?

LADY:—Uh-huh. Some drunk tourist made a fuss because I
wouldn't sell him no—liquor. . . .

NURSE [*crossing to the door*]: Oh. Mr. Torrance is sleeping
under medication.

LADY: That's good. [*She sits in shoe-fitting chair.*]

NURSE: I gave him a hypo at five.

LADY:—Don't all that morphine weaken the heart, Miss
Porter?

110

NURSE: Gradually, yes.

LADY: How long does it usually take for them to let go?

NURSE: It varies according to the age of the patient and the condition his heart's in. Why?

LADY: Miss Porter, don't people sort of help them let go?

NURSE: How do you mean, Mrs. Torrance?

LADY: Shorten their suffering for them?

NURSE: Oh, I see what you mean. [*Snaps her purse shut.*] —I see what you mean, Mrs. Torrance. But killing is killing, regardless of circumstances.

LADY: Nobody said killing.

NURSE: You said "shorten their suffering."

LADY: Yes, like merciful people shorten an animal's suffering when he's. . . .

NURSE: A human being is not the same as an animal, Mrs. Torrance. And I don't hold with what they call—

LADY [*overlapping*]: *Don't give me a sermon,* Miss Porter I just wanted to know if—

NURSE [*overlapping*]: I'm not giving a sermon. I just answered your question. If you want to get somebody to shorten your husband's life—

LADY [*jumping up; overlapping*]: Why, how dare you say that I—

NURSE: I'll be back at ten-thirty.

LADY: Don't!

NURSE: What?

LADY [*crossing behind counter*]: Don't come back at ten-thirty, don't come back.

111

NURSE: I'm always discharged by the doctors on my cases.

LADY: This time you're being discharged by the patient's wife.

NURSE: That's something we'll have to discuss with Dr. Buchanan.

LADY: I'll call him myself about it. I don't like you. I don't think you belong in the nursing profession, you have cold eyes; I think you like to watch pain!

NURSE: I know why you don't like my eyes. [*Snaps purse shut.*] You don't like my eyes because you know they see clear.

LADY: Why are you staring at *me?*

NURSE: I'm not staring at you, I'm staring at the curtain. There's something burning in there, smoke's coming out! [*Starts toward alcove.*] Oh.

LADY: Oh, no, you don't. [*Seizes her arm.*]

NURSE [*pushes her roughly aside and crosses to the curtain.* VAL *rises from cot, opens the curtain and faces her coolly*]: Oh, excuse me! [*She turns to* LADY.]—The moment I looked at you when I was called on this case last Friday morning I knew that you were pregnant.

[LADY *gasps.*]

I also knew the moment I looked at your husband it wasn't by him. [*She stalks to the door.* LADY *suddenly cries out:*]

LADY: Thank you for telling me what I hoped for is true.

MISS PORTER: You don't seem to have any shame.

LADY [*exalted*]: No. I don't have shame. I have—*great—joy!*

MISS PORTER [*venomously*]: Then why don't you get the calliope and the clown to make the announcement?

LADY: You do it for me, save me the money! Make the announcement, all over!

[NURSE *goes out.* VAL *crosses swiftly to the door and locks it. Then he advances toward her, saying:*]

VAL: Is it true what she said?

[LADY *moves as if stunned to the counter; the stunned look gradually turns to a look of wonder. On the counter is a heap of silver and gold paper hats and trumpets for the gala opening of the confectionery.*]

VAL [*in a hoarse whisper*]: Is it true or not true, what that woman told you?

LADY: You sound like a scared little boy.

VAL: She's gone out to tell.

[*Pause.*]

LADY: You gotta go now—it's dangerous for you to stay here. . . . Take your pay out of the cashbox, you can go. Go, go, take the keys to my car, cross the river into some other county. You've done what you came here to do. . . .

VAL:—It's true then, it's—?

LADY [*sitting in chair of counter*]: True as God's word! I have life in my body, this dead tree, my body, has burst in flower! You've given me life, you can go!

[*He crouches down gravely opposite her, gently takes hold of her knotted fingers and draws them to his lips, breathing on them as if to warm them. She sits bolt upright, tense, blind as a clairvoyant.*]

VAL:—Why didn't you tell me before?

LADY:—When a woman's been childless as long as I've been childless, it's hard to believe that you're still able to bear! —We used to have a little fig tree between the house and the

113

orchard. It never bore any fruit, they said it was barren. Time went by it, spring after useless spring, and it almost started to—die. . . . Then one day I discovered a small green fig on the tree they said wouldn't bear! [*She is clasping a gilt paper horn.*] I ran through the orchard. I ran through the wine garden shouting, "Oh, Father, it's going to bear, the fig tree is going to bear!"—It seemed such a wonderful thing, after those ten barren springs, for the little fig tree to bear, it called for a celebration—I ran to a closet, I opened a box that we kept Christmas ornaments in!—I took them out, glass bells, glass birds, tinsel, icicles, stars. . . . And I hung the little tree with them, I decorated the fig tree with glass bells and glass birds, and silver icicles and stars, because it won the battle and it would bear! [*Rises, ecstatic*] Unpack the box! Unpack the box with the Christmas ornaments in it, put them on me, glass bells and glass birds and stars and tinsel and snow! [*In a sort of delirium she thrusts the conical gilt paper hat on her head and runs to the foot of the stairs with the paper horn. She blows the horn over and over, grotesquely mounting the stairs, as* VAL *tries to stop her. She breaks away from him and runs up to the landing, blowing the paper horn and crying out:*] I've won, I've won, Mr. Death, I'm going to bear! [*Then suddenly she falters, catches her breath in a shocked gasp and awkwardly retreats to the stairs. Then turns screaming and runs back down them, her cries dying out as she arrives at the floor level. She retreats haltingly as a blind person, a hand stretched out to* VAL, *as slow, clumping footsteps and hoarse breathing are heard on the stairs. She moans:*]—Oh, God, oh —God. . . .

[JABE *appears on the landing, by the artificial palm tree in its dully lustrous green jardiniere, a stained purple robe hangs loosely about his wasted yellowed frame. He is death's self, and malignancy, as he peers, crouching, down into the store's dimness to discover his quarry.*]

114

JABE: Buzzards! Buzzards! [*Clutching the trunk of the false palm tree, he raises the other hand holding a revolver and fires down into the store.* LADY *screams and rushes to cover* VAL'S *motionless figure with hers.* JABE *scrambles down a few steps and fires again and the bullet strikes her, expelling her breath in a great "Hah!" He fires again; the great "Hah!" is repeated. She turns to face him, still covering* VAL *with her body, her face with all the passions and secrets of life and death in it now, her fierce eyes blazing, knowing, defying and accepting. But the revolver is empty; it clicks impotently and* JABE *hurls it toward them; he descends and passes them, shouting out hoarsely:*] I'll have you burned! I burned her father and I'll have you burned! [*He opens the door and rushes out onto the road, shouting hoarsely:*] The clerk is robbing the store, he shot my wife, the clerk is robbing the store, he killed my wife!

VAL:—Did it—?

LADY:—Yes!—it did. . . .

[*A curious, almost formal, dignity appears in them both. She turns to him with the sort of smile that people offer in apology for an awkward speech, and he looks back at her gravely, raising one hand as if to stay her. But she shakes her head slightly and points to the ghostly radiance of her make-believe orchard and she begins to move a little unsteadily toward it. Music.* LADY *enters the confectionery and looks about it as people look for the last time at a loved place they are deserting.*]

The show is over. The monkey is dead . . .

[*Music rises to cover whatever sound Death makes in the confectionery. It halts abruptly. Figures appear through the great front window of the store, pocket-lamps stare through the glass and someone begins to force the front door open.* VAL *cries out:*]

115

VAL: Which way!

[*He turns and runs through the dim radiance of the confectionery, out of our sight. Something slams. Something cracks open. Men are in the store and the dark is full of hoarse, shouting voices.*]

VOICES OF MEN [*shouting*]:—Keep to the walls! He's armed!

—Upstairs, Dog!

—Jack, the confectionery!

[*Wild cry back of store.*]

Got him. GOT HIM!

—They got him!

—Rope, git rope!

—Git rope from th' hardware section!

—I got something better than rope!

—What've you got?

—What's that, what's he got?

—A BLOWTORCH!

—Christ. . . .

[*A momentary hush.*]

—Come on, what in hell are we waiting for?

—Hold on a minute, I wanta see if it works!

—Wait, Wait!

—LOOK here!

[*A jet of blue flame stabs the dark. It flickers on CAROL'S figure in the confectionery. The men cry out together in*]

*hoarse passion crouching toward the fierce blue jet of fire,
their faces lit by it like the faces of demons.*]

—Christ!

—It works!

[*They rush out. Confused shouting behind. Motors start.
Fade quickly. There is almost silence, a dog bays in the
distance. Then—the* CONJURE MAN *appears with a bundle
of garments which he examines, dropping them all except
the snakeskin jacket, which he holds up with a toothless
mumble of excitement.*]

CAROL [*quietly, gently*]: What have you got there, Uncle?
Come here and let me see.

[*He crosses to her.*]

Oh yes, his snakeskin jacket. I'll give you a gold ring for it.

[*She slowly twists ring off her finger. Somewhere there is
a cry of anguish. She listens attentively till it fades out,
then nods with understanding.*]

—Wild things leave skins behind them, they leave clean
skins and teeth and white bones behind them, and these are
tokens passed from one to another, so that the fugitive kind
can always follow their kind. . . .

[*The cry is repeated more terribly than before. It expires
again. She draws the jacket about her as if she were cold,
nods to the old* NEGRO, *handing him the ring. Then she
crosses toward the door, pausing halfway as* SHERIFF
TALBOTT *enters with his pocket-lamp.*]

SHERIFF: Don't no one move, don't move!

[*She crosses directly past him as if she no longer saw him,
and out the door. He shouts furiously:*]

117

Stay here!

[*Her laughter rings outside. He follows the girl, shouting:*]

Stop! Stop!

[*Silence. The* NEGRO *looks up with a secret smile as the curtain falls slowly.*]

BATTLE OF ANGELS

Battle of Angels, a play in 2 acts and 3 scenes, was presented by the Theatre Guild, Inc., at the Wilbur Theatre, Boston, for two weeks, starting December 30, 1940, and ending January 11, 1941. Margaret Webster directed, the setting was by Cleon Throckmorton and the incidental music was by Colin McPhee, plus Negro spiritual recordings by H. F. Chalfin. No one is listed as lighting director in the program.

The Cast:

DOLLY BLAND	DOROTHY PETERSON
BEULAH CARTWRIGHT	EDITH KING
PEE WEE BLAND	ROBERT EMHARDT
SHERIFF TALBOTT	CHARLES McCLELLAND
CASSANDRA WHITESIDE	DORIS DUDLEY
VEE TALBOTT	KATHERINE RAHT
VALENTINE XAVIER	WESLEY ADDY
EVA TEMPLE	HAZEL HANNA
BLANCH TEMPLE	HELEN CAREWE
MYRA TORRANCE	MIRIAM HOPKINS
JOE	CLARENCE WASHINGTON
SMALL BOY	BERTRAM HOLMES
BENNIE	ICAN LEWIS
JABE TORRANCE	MARSHALL BRADFORD

PROLOGUE

SCENE: *A "mercantile" store in a very small and old-fashioned town in the Deep South. It has large windows facing a tired dirt road, across which is a gasoline pump, a broken-down wagon and cotton fields which extend to a cypress brake and the levee. The windows are shielded from sunlight by a tin portico so that the interior is rather dusky. The ceiling is very high and has two or three ceiling fans and old-fashioned lighting fixtures. There are a good many vertical lines which contribute to a dramatic atmosphere in the setting. In the back wall of the store is a steep flight of stairs leading up to the living quarters above. Left of this stairway is an open arch revealing a further room, the store's confectionery department.*

At the time this Prologue takes place—a Sunday afternoon about a year after the culmination of the tragedy—the store is no longer being run as a store, but has been converted into a museum exhibiting souvenirs of the sensational events which had taken place there. Various articles connected with the tragedy are on display, such as the snakeskin jacket, which is suspended in a conspicuous position. All these articles are labeled with crude hand-lettered signs.

An ancient Negro, the CONJURE MAN, *is dozing in a chair in the archway. There is an awesome dignity in his appearance, despite the grotesque touches of his costume. He is small and cadaverous, a wizard-like figure, with a double strand of bleached chicken or hawk bones strung about his neck, tiny bells sewn to his sleeves so that he makes a slight tinkling sound when he moves, and various other odd tokens or charms scattered about his garments, which he sells to the superstitious.*

[*There is a knock at the door.*]

WOMAN'S VOICE: Uncle! Uncle! [*The old* NEGRO *starts up. He rises and shuffles leisurely across to the door, unbolts it and draws it open on the mellow afternoon sunlight.* EVA *and* BLANCH TEMPLE *step inside.*]

EVA: Goodness . . .

BLANCH: Gracious sakes alive! It takes you forever to move a couple of inches. Come on in, folks! This is the famous Torrance Mercantile Store of Two Rivers, Mississippi. [*They are followed by a pair of middle-aged tourists.*]

EVA: Some people think it's sort of commercial of us to turn it into what the newspapers refer to as a Tragic Museum —but after all . . .

BLANCH: There's nothing else we can do to pay the taxes. Nobody would use this building for any other purpose, knowing what all happened in here once.

EVA: Not that it's haunted, but . . .

BLANCH: It's full of shadows. Electric power's cut off. Needless expense.

EVA: Electric power was off at the time it happened.

BLANCH: The power always goes off when it rains real hard and that Good Friday was one of the heaviest rains we've had in Two Rivers County.

EVA: Miss Harkaway called it a cataclysm of nature.

BLANCH: She was that wonderful Memphis newspaper-woman who wrote it all up in the *Commercial Appeal*.

EVA: Everything's just as it was.

BLANCH: Except of course the merchandise was removed.

EVA: Nothing has been took out that had a connection.

122

BLANCH: Everything in the museum has a label on it. You all can just browse around and we'll explain everything.

EVA: How can they ask any questions, you talking so fast?

BLANCH: You get me all balled up with your interruptions! Now that over there is the famous Jesus picture!

EVA: Don't call it *that.*

BLANCH: That's what *everyone* calls it. He *was* good-looking.

EVA: I never noticed he was.

BLANCH: Don't be ridiculous. *Everyone* noticed he was.

EVA: Now that dress there is the dress that Myra was wearing. Beulah said to her, "What do they call that color?"

BLANCH: She smiled an' she said, "They call it ecstasy blue!" Then didn't Myra . . . ?

EVA: Myra went back upstairs. Jabe knocked on the ceiling. That was when Vee . . .

BLANCH: Never mind about that. We'll tell that later. There is the phone . . .

EVA: The receiver is still off the hook.

BLANCH: The cashbox drawer's still open.

EVA: The money has been removed.

BLANCH [*regretfully*]: There *wasn't* much.

EVA: Frightfully, frightfully *little*. We are the only surviving relations, of course.

BLANCH [*pointing to the floor*]: You see those stains?

EVA: They're fading out. We'll have to touch them up.

BLANCH: Across the floor? Toward the confectionery?

123

EVA: Let's go in there! [*She rushes eagerly forward.*] Uncle, the *lamp!*

BLANCH: You probably wonder why we put up with such a peculiar old man as the caretaker here. Well, it's like this . . .

EVA: He's part of the exhibition!

BLANCH: Don't call it that!

EVA: Oh, the memorial then! What's the difference? This Conjure Man, as they call him . . .

BLANCH: Comes from Blue Mountain. Myra gave him odd jobs.

EVA: He was on the place when everything happened that happened.

BLANCH: He claims he knows some things that he isn't telling.

EVA: He's kind of daft. Now this room here is the Torrance Confectionery. Myra had it all done over for spring.

BLANCH: Yes, redecorated. Somebody made a remark how lovely it was. "Yes," said Myra, "it's supposed to resemble the orchard across from Moon Lake!" Notice those imitations . . .

EVA: Dogwood blossoms. And that big Japanese lantern. It's dingy now but you all can just imagine how lovely it was.

BLANCH: Miss Harkaway put it in such a beautiful way. The mercantile store, she said, was reality, harsh and drab, but Myra's confectionery . . .

EVA: That was where she kept her dreams. Uncle, turn up that lamp. I want these people to see the place where she kept her dreams. [*The lamp is turned up higher. The confectionery blooms into a nostalgic radiance, as dim and soft as memory itself.*] Remind me, Blanch, to sprinkle a little roach powder on this floor.

EVA: Let's go upstairs.

BLANCH: I think we've left out something.

EVA: You can talk so fast I didn't keep track of it all.

BLANCH: It's you with your interruptions that ball things up. Watch out for these stairs, they're terrible, terrible steep.

EVA: We can't be responsible for an accident on them.

BLANCH: Goodness sakes alive, *no!* These terrible taxes . . .

EVA: Keep us poor as church mice! [*They lead the way up the stairs.*]

BLANCH: You keep awake, Uncle.

EVA: If anyone else stops in, just ring the bell.

BLANCH [*opening the door on the landing*]: Now these are the living quarters.

EVA: Myra's bedroom's on the right an' Jabe's on the left.

[*The light fades out as the door closes. The* CONJURE MAN *laughs to himself as the curtain falls.*]

ACT ONE

SCENE: *The same as for the Prologue, except that it is now a year earlier—in early February—and the store is in operation, stocked with merchandise. There are great bolts of pepperel and percale which stand upright on the counters. The black skeleton of a dressmaker's dummy stands meaninglessly in front of a thin white column. Along the wall at the left is the shoe department, with a ladder that slides along the shelves and two or three shoe-fitting chairs. Racks of dresses, marked "Spring Styles," line the right wall.*

DOLLY *and* BEULAH *are arranging candles and setting a buffet table in the general store. They are wives of small planters, about thirty and overdressed.* DOLLY'S *husband,* PEE WEE, *and the town* SHERIFF *are in the confectionery shooting pinball. A train whistles in the distance.*

DOLLY: Pee Wee! That's the Cannonball!

PEE WEE [*from the confectionery*]: Okay, Mama! [PEE WEE *enters. He is a heavy man. His vest comes midway down the white-shirted bulge of his belly; his laced boots are caked with mud.*] Ninety-five nickles an' no pay-off! What would you call that, Mama?

DOLLY: Outrageous! Not the machine, but you poor suckers that play it.

BEULAH: This meringue turned out real good.

SHERIFF [*entering from the confectionery, laughing*]: You got to mid-aisle it three times straight's the only way to crack that goddam pot.

PEE WEE: I'm gonna tell Jabe about it. Ninety-five nickels an' no pay-off. [*They go out.*]

DOLLY: I guess Jabe Torrance has got more to think about than that ole pinball game in the confectionery. Huh?

126

BEULAH: He ought to have. That meringue *is* nice and light. I put in two drops of almond. Yesterday I was talking to Dr. Bob. You know, young Dr. Bob?

DOLLY: Uh-huh. What did he say?

BEULAH: I ast him how Jabe was, what kind of condition he really seemed to be in. He's seen them X-ray pictures they took in the Memphis Hospital after the operation. Well . . .

DOLLY: What did he say, Beulah?

BEULAH: He said the worst that a doctor can ever say.

DOLLY: What's that?

BEULAH: Nothing at all, not a spoken word did he utter; he simply looked at me with those big dark eyes and shook his haid—like this!

DOLLY [*speaking with doleful optimism*]: I guess he signed Jabe Torrance's death warrant with just that single motion of his haid.

BEULAH: Exackly what I thought. I understand that they cut him open . . .

DOLLY: An' sewed him right back up?

BEULAH [*struggling to speak and strangling on an olive*]: Mmm. Mmm. [*She points at her stuffed mouth.*] I didn't know these olives had seeds in them.

DOLLY: You thought they was stuffed?

BEULAH: Uh-huh.

DOLLY: Where's the Temple Sisters?

BEULAH: Snooping around upstairs.

DOLLY: Let Myra catch 'em at it, she'll lay 'em both out good. She never did invite nobody up there.

BEULAH: Well, I was surprised when I went up myself.

127

DOLLY: I know it.

BEULAH: Two separate bedrooms, too! Maybe it's just since Jabe's been sick.

DOLLY: Naw, it's permanent, honey. As a girl in Tupelo she certainly wasn't cold-blooded. We used to go double together me an' Pee Wee an' her and that Anderson boy. All of one spring we would go to the orchard across from Moon Lake ev'ry night. We was engaged, but they wasn't. Boll weevil and army-worm struck his cotton awful three times straight. He married into the Delta Planters' Bank and Myra married Jabe. Myra was Myra then. Since then she's just a woman that works in a mercantile store.

[CASSANDRA WHITESIDE *enters at the door on the right. She is dark and strikingly beautiful, of a type rather peculiar to the South—physically delicate with clear translucent skin and luminous eyes as though burnt thin by her intensity of feeling. With people she has a rather disdainful ease, not deliberate or conscious, but rooted in her class origin and the cynical candor with which she recognizes herself and the social contradictions and tragic falsity of the world she lives in.* SANDRA *is the only woman of aristocratic extraction in the group. Her family is the oldest in this part of the Delta and was once the richest, but their plantation has dwindled with each successive generation.* SANDRA *has been "going out" for ten years and is still unmarried, which is enough in itself to destroy a girl's reputation.*]

DOLLY: Sandra Whiteside! How are you?

SANDRA: Oh, I seem to be still living. God knows why. Where's Myra?

DOLLY: Gone to Memphis to bring Jabe back from the hospital.

BEULAH: The men folks just now went to the depot to meet them.

SANDRA: Oh. . . . I want some cartridges for this pistol of mine. [*She removes it from her bag.*] I thought I better carry one with me. I'm on the road so much you'd think I was making a political campaign tour, the number of places I've got to visit this weekend. Memphis, Jackson— Is this the hardware section? [*approaching the counter*] Aw, here's cartridges! [*She helps herself.*] Then on down to New Awleuns for the start of the carnival season. Tell Myra to charge these to me. I ought to buy an airplane. They say that you only crack up once in the air.

DOLLY: Well, you'd better stay out of airplanes, honey.

BEULAH: How many times have you cracked up on the highway?

SANDRA: Today was the seventh since New Year's.

DOLLY: No!

SANDRA: I fell asleep at the wheel an' ran into a fence.

BEULAH: Goodness!

DOLLY: Gracious!

BEULAH: Last week she had a collision with a mule.

DOLLY: My Lawd!

SANDRA: And just to show you the absolute lack of justice, the mule was killed and I was completely uninjured!

DOLLY [*with false concern*]: Darling, you'd better be careful!

SANDRA: Oh, I don't know. What else can you do when you live in Two River County but drive like hell! [*There is the sound of a car out in front.*]

BEULAH: 'S 'at them?

DOLLY [*sarcastically*]: Naw, it's the Sheriff's little fireside companion.

BEULAH: Vee Talbott! Who is that with her? A *man!* [*This word creates a visible stir among the three women.*]

DOLLY: Uh-huh! Yes, it is!

BEULAH: Who could it be I wonder?

DOLLY: I can't make out. Oh, my goodness! What an outfit he's got on! It looks like a snakeskin jacket.

BEULAH: *Wha-at?* Do you know him?

DOLLY: Naw, I don't know him a-tall. He looks like an absolute stranger. Poor Vee has got her skirt caught in the car door or something, it's hitched up over her knees and she's simply *frantic* about it! [*She utters a sharp laugh.*]

BEULAH: She's such a big clumsy thing. Who do you think the man is?

DOLLY: I told you I never have seen him, don't know him from Adam, darling. Maybe he's one of the Twelve Apostles that she's been painting on.

SANDRA: Is Vee painting the Twelve Apostles?

DOLLY: She's been painting them for twelve years, one each year. She says that she sees them in visions. But every one of them looks like some man around Two River County. She told Birdie Wilson that she was hoping she'd have a vision of Jesus next Passion Week so she could paint Him, too.

BEULAH: You better quit staring.

DOLLY: She's finally got her skirt loose. Oh, God, the hem's ripped out, it's trailing the ground! [*She laughs and crosses from the window.*]

[VEE *enters from the street. She is a heavy, middle-aged woman, about forty, whose personality, frustrated in its contact with externals, has turned deeply inward. She has found refuge in religion and primitive art and has become known as an eccentric. Although a religious fanatic, a mystic, she should not be made ridiculous. Her portrayal will contain certain incidents of humor, but not be devoid of all dignity or pathos. She wanders slowly about with a vague dreamy smile on her face. Her expression is often bewildered.*]

BEULAH [*with loud, false cordiality*]: Hello, Vee honey, how are you?

DOLLY: Hello, Vee.

VEE [*faintly*]: Hello. I got m' skirt caught in the lock of the Chevrolet door an' I think it's torn loose a little. I can't see behind me good. Does it look like it's torn to you? [*She peers awkwardly, ponderously, behind her at the hem which dangles across the floor, like a big heavy dog trying to catch its tail.*]

BEULAH: Just a little bit, honey.

DOLLY: Yes, it's scarcely noticeable even. [*She giggles.*]

VEE: I feel like something was dragging. Oh, it *has* been torn, the young man told me it wasn't!

DOLLY: Say, who is he?

VEE: I don't know who he is, but I think he's all right, though. He told me he'd been saved, doesn't smoke, doesn't drink. His parents are dead, both of them, but he's got an uncle who's a Catholic priest and he says that he stayed six years—I mean his uncle—in some leper colony on a South Sea island without ever catching any sign of disease. Isn't that wonderful, though?

DOLLY: Huh.

BEULAH: What's he doing here?

131

VEE: Says he's exploring the world an' ev'rything in it.

DOLLY: Laudamighty!

VEE: He come to the lockup las' night an' ast for a bed, but he couldn't stay in it, though, the bars made him nervous.

DOLLY: So what did you do with him then?

VEE: What do you mean? I was alone in the house so I give him a blanket; he went out to sleep in his car.

DOLLY: Sounds like a peculiar person.

BEULAH: Yeah.

VEE: Oh, no, he just isn't a type that you are used to seeing. I'm going to speak a good word for him to Myra, she said she might be needing some help around here. [VAL *appears in the front door. He is about twenty-five years old. He has a fresh and primitive quality, a virile grace and freedom of body, and a strong physical appeal.*] Come right on in, Mr. Xavier.

VAL: What shall I do with this here?

VEE: Jus' give me the sherbet. I thought Mr. Torrance might need somethin' light an' digestible so I brought sherbet.

BEULAH: What flavuh is it? Pineapple?

VEE: Pineapple.

BEULAH: Oh, goody, I love pineapple. Don't you-all? [*She hands* VEE *the napkin-wrapped bowl.*]

VEE: Mr. Xavier, I was just telling these ladies about your uncle that went to live with the lepers. Some people are doubtful about the power of faith but there's an example I think should convince anybody.

BEULAH: Isn't it, though? Let's put this right in the Frigidaire before it stahts t' melt.

DOLLY [*lifting the napkin*]: I'm afraid you're locking the stable after the hause is gone.

BEULAH: Wh-at? Is it melted awready?

DOLLY: Reduced to juice!

BEULAH: Oh foot!—Well, let's put it in anyhow, it might thicken up.

VEE: Where is the Frigidaire?

BEULAH: It's in the confectionery. [*The three women go back through the archway.* SANDRA *is left with* VAL. *She laughs in her throat and leans provocatively back.* VAL *stares at her with a touch of antagonism. This challenging silence continues for a marked pause. Then* SANDRA *laughs again, somewhat louder.*]

VAL [*sharply*]: Is something amusing you, lady?

SANDRA [*drawling*]: Yes, very much. I think it's that jacket you're wearing. What stuff is it made of?

VAL: Snakeskin.

SANDRA [*with a disgusted grimace*]: Ouuu!

VAL: I didn't ask your opinion.

SANDRA: I didn't express one, did I?

VAL: Yeah. You said "Ouuu!" [*He mocks her grimace.*]

SANDRA: You know what that was? It was fascinated revulsion. [*She goes into the confectionery and starts the juke box. It plays "Custro Vidas."*] Would you like to dance?

VAL: I don't know how to dance.

SANDRA: I'd love to teach you. We'll go out jooking some night.

VAL: Jooking? What's that?

SANDRA: That's where you get in a car and drink a little and drive a little and dance a little. Then you drink a little more and drive a little more and dance a little more. Then you stop dancing and just drink and drive. Then you stop driving and you just drink. And then, finally, you stop drinking.

VAL: Then what do you do?

SANDRA: That depends entirely on who you happen to be out jooking with. If you're out with me, and you're sufficiently attractive, you nearly always wind up on Cypress Hill.

VAL: What's that?

SANDRA: That's the graveyard, honey. It's situated, appropriately enough, on the highest point of land in Two River County, a beautiful windy bluff just west of the Sunflower River.

VAL: Why do you go out there?

SANDRA: Because dead people give such good advice.

VAL: What advice do they give?

SANDRA: Just one word—*live!* [BEULAH *rushes in with a bowl of something.*]

BEULAH: You're going to stay fo' the pahty, Mr. . . . ?

VAL: Xavier.

BEULAH: I know some Seviers in Blue Mountain. Any relation?

VAL: Spelt with an "S" or an "X"?

BEULAH: An "S," I believe.

VAL: No relation.

BEULAH [*sympathetically*]: Awwww. [*She rushes back out.*]

134

SANDRA: I have a great aunt who's laid away on Cypress Hill. Her name was Cassandra, the same as mine is, so I always empty my bottles on her grave. She loved to drink. She finally got so she just lay on the bed and drank and drank all night and all day. They asked her if she didn't get tired of it. She said, "No, I never get bored. I have moving pictures on my ceiling. They go on all the time, continuous performance. I'm the main actress," she said, "and I do the most mah-velous things!" That was Cassandra the second. I'm the third. The first was a little Greek girl who slept in the shrine of Apollo. Her ears were snake-bitten, like mine, so that she could understand the secret language of the birds. You know what they told her, Snakeskin? They contradicted everything that she'd been told before. They said it was all stuff an' nonsense, a pack of lies. They advised her to drive her car as fast as she wanted to drive it, to dance like she wanted to dance. Get drunk, they said, raise hell at Moon Lake casina, do bumps an' wiggle your fanny! [VEE TALBOT *enters; she stops short with an outraged look.* SANDRA *laughs and extends a pack of cigarettes toward* VAL.]

VEE: Mr. Xavier don't smoke. [*She sets the potato chips down and goes out.*]

DOLLY [*rushing through*]: Mr. Xavier, if you're looking for work, you might drop in on my husband, Pee Wee Bland. He runs that cotton gin right over the road there.

BEULAH: The marguerites! I smell them burning! [*She runs out.*]

SANDRA: How did you happen to come to this dark, wild river country of ours?

VAL: A broken axle stopped me here last night.

SANDRA: You'd better mend it quick and move along.

VAL: Why's that?

135

SANDRA: Why? Why? Don't you know what those women are suffering from: Sexual malnutrition! They look at you with eyes that scream "Eureka!" [*She laughs and saunters casually to the door. She raises her revolver and fires two shots into the sky.*]

VAL: For God's sake! [*The three women scream and come rushing back in. The* TEMPLE SISTERS *shriek upstairs and come scuttling down,* BLANCH *losing her footing and sliding down the last three steps. There is babble and confusion.*]

DOLLY: What are you *doing?* Oh, God, in my condition! I . . .

BEULAH: Sandra, for the love of . . .

BLANCH [*moaning*]: I've broke my laig in two!

EVA [*screaming*]: She's broken her laig! [VEE *goes over to her.*]

DOLLY: Oh, she has *not!* Sandra, what on earth did you fire that damn thing faw?

SANDRA [*laughs and comes unsteadily back into the store*]: I took a pot shot at a buzzard!

BEULAH: A what? [SANDRA *laughs wildly and looks at* VAL, *who crosses to her and takes the pistol roughly from her grasp.* MYRA *enters.* MYRA *is a slight, fair woman, about thirty-four years old. She is a woman who met emotional disaster in her girlhood and whose personality bears traces of the resulting trauma. Frequently sharp and suspicious, she verges on hysteria under slight strain. Her voice is often shrill and her body tense. But when in repose, a girlish softness emerges—evidence of her capacity for great tenderness.*]

MYRA: What in God's holy name has been going on here? Who fired those shots out the door? [*She sees* VAL *with the revolver in his hand; she gasps and starts toward the door.*] You! [*They stare at each other for a brief moment.*]

VAL [*slowly smiling*]: No ma'am, it wasn't me. It was this young lady here.

SANDRA: Yes, I fired it, darling.

MYRA: What at?

SANDRA: A bird of ill omen was circling over the store.

MYRA: Yea? One of those imaginary things that people see in a certain condition. Hello, Beulah, Dolly. [*She flings off her hat.*] I'm evermore tired. I've never had such a trip. Jabe took a bad spell on the train. They carried him up the back way. How are yuh, Vee. Blanch Temple, what are you sitting on the floor faw?

EVA: She took a spill on the stairs when Sandra Whiteside fired the shots!

MYRA: On the stairs? You two were upstairs, were you?

EVA: Yes, we were straightening things up a little . . .

MYRA [*quickly*] I see. An investigation?

EVA: Yes. I mean . . .

BLANCH: No, no, no! We wanted to see that ev'rything was in order. I've got such awful weak ankles, I'm always tripping and falling. An' I've got to march in church with the choir if I got to go on crutches. [*She rises painfully with* BEULAH'S *and* EVA'S *assistance.*]

MYRA: Oh, look what you all have done, that beautiful table! Candles an' ev'rything sweet that goes to make a nice party! Some of your lovely floating island, Beulah? Sweet! The spirit is willing but the flesh is completely exhausted. [*A Negro enters, crosses to* MYRA *carrying a tower of pastel-colored hatboxes and a big gay placard reading* "Welcome Sweet Springtime."] Oh, Joe, bring me those cards. Welcome sweet springtime! I've bought a pile of spring hats. [*She*

137

extricates one of the cards.] This one here is the nicest—"In the spring, a young maid's fancy lightly turns to new chapeaux."

BEULAH [*reading the rest of it*]: "Mary Lou and Jane and Frances wear new hats to please their beaux!"

DOLLY: Oh, that's perfectly dahling. It seems so eahly, though, to think about spring.

EVA: I don't know. Somebody tole me that carps have been seen in Yazoo Pass. That always indicates that flood season's 'bout to start.

BLANCH: Myra . . .

MYRA: Yes?

BLANCH: I don't suppose you feel like talkin' about it right now, but I do hope Jabe's operation was completely successful.

MYRA: No.

BLANCH: It wasn't? [*All the women stare greedily at* MYRA.]

MYRA: No. It *wasn't.*

BLANCH: Oh!

EVA: My! My!

BEULAH: I'm so sorry to hear it.

DOLLY: If there's anything I can do . . . I—? [JABE *is heard knocking on the ceiling from his room above.* MYRA'S *face becomes suddenly listless and tired.*]

EVA: What's that knocking upstairs?

MYRA: Jabe.

SHERIFF [*calling from above*]: Myra, Jabe wants you.

MYRA: Excuse me, I'll have to go up. [*She crosses wearily toward the stairs, her hat dangling from one hand, pauses be-*

138

fore the "Welcome Sweet Springtime" *sign, with its bluebirds, flutes and gilded scrolls and cherubim, gravely lifts it and places it in a higher position.*] Dolly, look at this hat! I think it must have been created just for you! [*She smiles and goes on upstairs.*]

SANDRA [*who has engaged* VAL *in low conversation since* MYRA'S *entrance*]: Speaking of knocks, I've got one in my engine. A very mysterious noise. I can't decide whether I'm in communication with one of my dead ancestors or whether the carburetor or something is just about to drop out an' leave me stranded, probably at midnight in the middle of some lonesome black forest! [*She smiles at* VAL.] I don't suppose you'd have any knowledge of mechanics?

VAL: I dunno. I might. [DOLLY *is trying on the hat but is watchful of this exchange—also the other women who are opening hatboxes.*]

SANDRA: Would you be willing to undertake a kind of exploratory operation on it?

VAL: Well, I might if it didn't take too long.

SANDRA [*drawling*]: Oh, with your expert knowledge it shouldn't take lo-ong at-all! [DOLLY *giggles.*]

DOLLY: This hat! Isn't it the strangest thing?

BEULAH: Them things on the brim—what are they—carrots an' peas? I think they'd be much better *creamed*—with chicken croquettes! [VAL *has slid slowly off the counter. He moves past* SANDRA *and the secret looks of the women, toward the door.*]

VEE: Mr. Xavier . . . [*She crosses as if to stop him but they have already disappeared.*] Oh, I was going to ask Myra if she would give him a job.

BEULAH: Well . . .

139

DOLLY: It looks like he's *got* one now!

EVA: What did she say? A knock . . . ?

BLANCH: In her engine! [*innocently*] Whatever that is.

DOLLY [*with a peal of laughter*]: Did you *evuh* see such a puh-faum-ance! *Nevuh* in all my . . .

BEULAH: Bawn days? *Neither* did I! You see how she looked at the boy? An' the tone of huh voice. Corrupt? Absolutely—de-*grad-ed!*

DOLLY: Hank says her father got drunk one time at the Elks an' told him that she was kicked out of both of those girls' schools. Had to send her out East where morals don't matter. She's got two degrees or something in *lit-*era-*chure.*

BEULAH: Six degrees of fever if you ask me!

VEE [*who has been silently brooding over the situation*]: I certainly hope she doesn't get him to drink.

DOLLY: Vee, honey, you might as well face it, this is one candidate fo' salvation that you have *lost* to the opposition!

VEE: I don't believe it. He told me that he'd been saved already. [*She fixes her resentment on* DOLLY.] If some of the older women in Two River County would set a better example there'd be more justice in their talk about girls!

DOLLY [*with asperity*]: What do you mean by that remark?

VEE: I mean that people who give drinkin' pahties an' get so drunk they don't know which is *their husband* an' which is somebody else's an' people who serve on the altar guild an' still play cards on Sundays . . .

DOLLY: Just stop right there! Now I've discovered the source of that dirty gossip!

VEE: I'm only repeating what I've been told by others! I certainly never have been entertained at such affairs as that!

140

DOLLY: No, an' you never will be; you're a public kill-joy, a professional hypocrite!

BEULAH: Dolly!

DOLLY: She spends her time re-fauming tramps that her husband puts in the *lockup!* Brings them here in Myra's store an' tries to get them jobs here when God knows what kind of vicious ideas they've probably got in their heads!

VEE: I try to build up characters! You an' your drinkin' pahties are only concerned with tearin' characters down! I'm goin' upstairs with Myra. [*She goes out.*]

DOLLY: Well, you know what brought on that tantrum? She's jealous of Sandra Whiteside's running off with that strange boy. She hasn't lived as a natural wife for ten years or more [*to* EVA] so her husband has got to pick up with some bright-skinned nigger.

BEULAH: Oh, Dolly, you're awful. Sometimes I think you ought to wear a backhouse on your haid instead of a hat.

DOLLY: I've got no earthly patience with that sort of hypo-criticism. Beulah, let's put all this perishable stuff in the Frigidaire and get out of here. I've never been so thoroughly disgusted.

BEULAH: Oh, my Lawd! [*They go into the confectionery.*]

EVA: Both of those two women are as common as dirt.

BLANCH: Dolly's folks in Blue Mountain are nothin' at all but the poorest kind of white trash. Why, Lollie Tucker told me the old man sits on the porch with his shoes off drinkin' beer out of a bucket! Nobody wants these marguerites. [*She goes to the hardware counter and gets her bag.*] Let's take 'em, huh?

EVA [*looking at the flowers*]: I was just wondering what we'd use to decorate the altar with tomorrow. The Bishop

141

Adjutant's comin'. As far's I know nobody's offered flowers. We can give Myra credit in the Parish notes.

BLANCH: Put the olive-nut sandwiches in here with the marguerites. Be careful you tote them so they won't get squashed.

EVA: They'll come in very nicely for the Bishop's tea. [DOLLY *and* BEULAH *re-enter from the confectionery.*]

DOLLY: We still have time to make the second show.

BEULAH: Dolly, you still have on that awful hat!

DOLLY: Oh, Lawd! [*She tosses it on the counter.* DOLLY *and* BEULAH *go out quickly together.*]

EVA [*when they are out*]: Sits on the po'ch with his shoes off?

BLANCH: Yes! Drinkin' *beer* from a *bucket!* [EVA *and* BLANCH *go out. The* SHERIFF *comes downstairs, grunting and puffing, followed by* PEE WEE.]

PEE WEE: Took one dose at noon. When that didn't work, I took a double one about five o'clock. Jabe sure looks bad.

SHERIFF: Looks no better 'n no worse 'n he always looked, but if what they say is correct, he'll more'n likely go under before the cotton comes up! See that there? [*He indicates his bandaged knuckle.*] Broke my knuckle! Never hit a bucktooth nigger in the mouf! That's *the moral of it.* [PEE WEE *laughs.*] Oh, Vee! . . . Them fool wimmin got in a ruckus down here, I don't know what it's about. [VEE *comes downstairs.*]

VEE: Hush that bawling will yuh! I wanted to speak with Myra about that young man who needs work but I couldn't in front of Jabe. He thinks he's gonna be able to go back to work himself.

SHERIFF: Well, come awn here, quit foolin'!

VEE: I think I ought to wait 'till that young man gets back.

SHERIFF: Mama, you come awn. Aw else stay here, an' *walk* when you git ready. [*He strides out after* PEE WEE. *The car engine roars.* VEE *looks troubled and follows them slowly out. There is a slight pause. The* NEGRO *enters from the confectionery. He looks about him and laughs with a gentle, quiet laughter at something secret, opens the soft drink cooler and takes a coke out. He laughs again, softly, secretly, and goes out the front door of the store, leaving the door open. A hound bays in the distance. After a moment* VAL *comes back in, and shuts the door behind him. He goes to the table, picks up a paper napkin and scrubs lipstick off his mouth. He settles himself on the counter. After a moment or two* MYRA *comes downstairs bearing an oil lamp. She has on a cheap Japanese kimono of shiny black satin with large scarlet poppies on it. She appears to be very distraught and doesn't notice* VAL. *She crosses directly to the phone and turns the crank.*]

MYRA: Get me the drugstore, please. Mr. Dubinsky? This is Myra Torrance. Were you asleep? I'm sorry. I'm in a bad situation. I left my Luminal tablets in the Memphis hotel and I can't sleep without them. . . . I know your store's closed up. So's mine. I know the lights are out, they're out over here. But you don't need a thousand watt bulb to put a few Luminal tablets in a little cardboard box or paper bag. . . . Now look here, Mr. Dubinsky, if you want to keep my trade, you send your nigger right over with that box of tablets. Gone? Then bring 'em yourself! I'm absolutely desperate from lack of sleep. My nerves are all on edge. If I don't get a good sleep tonight, I'll go all to pieces. I've got a sick man to take care of. . . . Yes, I just brought him home from the Memphis

143

hospital. The operation was not at all successful. Will you do that? I'll be very much obliged. Thank you, Mr. Dubinsky. Excuse me for speaking so sharply. Thank you, Mr. Dubinsky. I appreciate that, Mr. Dubinsky. Goodbye, Mr. Dubinsky. [*She hangs up the phone and leans exhaustedly against the wall.*] Oh, oh, oh, I wish I was dead—dead—dead.

VAL [*quietly*]: No, you don't, Mrs. Torrance.

MYRA: My God! [*She gasps and clutches her wrapper about her throat.*]

VAL: I didn't mean to scare you.

MYRA: *What is this?* What are you still doing here? Who *are you?* My God, you got eyes that shine in the dark like a dog's. Get out or I'll call for the Sheriff!

VAL: Lady . . .

MYRA: Well?

VAL: I've been to the Sheriff's already.

MYRA: Aw. Escaped from the lockup?

VAL: Naw. The Sheriff's wife took me in there last night.

MYRA: She did, uh?

VAL: She give me a night's flop there but I didn't stay.

MYRA: Naw?

VAL: It made me uneasy being locked up. I got to have space around me.

MYRA: Look here, that's interesting, but this store's closed and I'll thank you to please get out. I've got a sick man upstairs that requires a lot of attention. If you're hungry . .

VAL: I'm not.

MYRA: There's lots of fancy stuff they put in the Frigidaire, you might as well eat it, I can't.

144

VAL: No, thanks, but I'd be mighty obliged if you would give me a job.

MYRA: There's no work here.

VAL: Excuse the contradiction but there is. Mizz Talbott told me so.

MYRA: Vee Talbott? I'll thank her to let me decide such things for myself. I'm in the mercantile business, she's a painter of very peculiar pictures she calls the Apostles but look like men around town. She took you in, did she? Well!

VAL: Whatever it is you're suggesting is incorrect. I've met one bitch in this town but it wasn't her.

MYRA [*furiously*]: How—how—*dare* you say that!

VAL: It wasn't you neither, ma'am! It was one that picked me up in here before you come in. Said she had engine trouble and would I fix it. She took me for a stud—and I slapped her face!

MYRA: You *what?*

VAL: I said I slapped her face. She wasn't a bad piece neither but I didn't like the way she went about it, like she was something special and I was trash!

MYRA: You . . . Cassandra Whiteside? *Slapped?* [*She bursts into wild laughter.*] I've never heard anything so beautiful in all my life! Have a drink and get out; I've got to go up.

VAL [*stubbornly*]: You'll need help here with your husband sick upstairs.

MYRA: You think so, uh? Well, if I do it'll have to be local help. I couldn't hire no stranger. 'Specially one that slapped the face of one of the richest girls in the Mississippi Delta. [*She laughs again.*] You had sales experience?

VAL: I've had all kinds of experience.

145

MYRA: That's not what I ast you. I ast you if you've had experience in the mercantile line. I want to know if you would be able to sell?

VAL: Sell?

MYRA: Yes!

VAL: Lots in hell to preachers!

MYRA [*utters again that sharp startled laugh, her fingers tightly clutching a magazine and nervously turning through it*]: I guess you got character ref'rence?

VAL: Sure.

MYRA: Where was the last place you worked?

VAL: Garage in Oakley.

MYRA: Tennessee?

VAL: Yeah.

MYRA: Grease-monkey, was you?

VAL [*stiffly*]: I wouldn't call myself that.

MYRA: Excuse me. Why did you quit that job?

VAL: If I told you, you'd think I was crazy.

MYRA: I think ev'rybody is crazy, including myself. Why did you quit it?

VAL: The place next door burnt down.

MYRA: What's that got to do with it?

VAL: I don't like fire. I dreamed about it three nights straight so I quit. I was burnt as a kid and ever since then it's been something I can't forget. [*He offers her a paper.*] Here's a letter he wrote:

MYRA: Who?

VAL: Garage manager.

MYRA [*reading aloud*]: "This here boy's peculiar but he sure does work real hard and he's honest as daylight." What does he mean "peculiar"?

VAL: Unusual is what he means.

MYRA: Why don't he say unusual?

VAL: He's not exactly an expert in the use of the language.

MYRA: Oh, but you are?

VAL [*removing a small book from his pocket*]: See this?

MYRA: Funk and Wagnall's Pocket Dictionary.

VAL: I carry that along with me wherever I go.

MYRA: What for?

VAL: You ever seen a coal-miner's cap? [MYRA *shakes her head.*] I wore one once when I was mining in the Red Hills of Alabama. It had a little lamp in front so you could see what your pick was digging into. Well—I'm still digging.

MYRA: Digging?

VAL: I don't claim to know very much, but I am writing a *book*.

MYRA: Well—you don't have to spit in my face to convince me of it!

VAL [*grinning*]: Excuse me.

MYRA: What's your book about?

VAL: Life.

MYRA: Sorry, but I can't use you.

VAL: Why not?

MYRA: Other people ain't as charitable as that garage manager is. They wouldn't say "peculiar," they'd say "nuts!" Also your appearance is much against you.

147

VAL: What's wrong with that.

MYRA: I don't know exactly. If you're hungry, eat. But otherwise . . . [*She is interrupted by knocking on the ceiling.*] Otherwise . . . get out. I'm too bone-tired to carry on conversation.

VAL: If you'll excuse me for telling you so, you're just about the rudest talking woman I've ever met.

MYRA: Yes, I'm mean inside. You heard me cussing when I come downstairs? Inside I cuss like that all the time. I hate ev'rybody; I wish this town would be bombarded tomorrow and everyone daid. Because—

VAL: Because?

MYRA: I got to live in it when I'd rather be daid in it— an' buried. [*She takes a drink of wine.*] What I meant about your appearance is you're too good-looking. Can you read shoe sizes?

VAL: Yeah.

MYRA: What does 75 David mean? [VAL *is stymied.*] You see how you lie? You lie like a dawg in summer! [*She laughs, not unkindly.*] 75 means 7½ in length and David means D wide. For flat-footed wimmin. You would either scare trade out of this store completely or else you'd bring it in so thick the floor would collapse. I can't decide which it would be.

VAL: I'd bring it in, lady.

MYRA: Gosh—[*There is a knock at the front door.* MYRA *crosses to it.*] A new floor would be an awful expense! [*She opens the door and steps outside.*] Thank you, Mr. Dubinsky. [*coming back in*] That was the sandman with my Luminal tablets. Suppose you—[*She opens the box and places a tablet on her tongue, washing it down with wine.*]

VAL: Huh?

MYRA: Suppose you try to sell me a pair of white kid pumps out of that new stock there. Imagine me a customer hard to please and you the clerk. Go on. . . . Naw, them over there is Red Goose shoes for kiddies. Them're men's shoes. Growing girls', misses'. Them on the end of the shelves are women's; sizes range down from the top. [*He pulls out a pair.*] You call them kid? That's suede, young man; 'snot a pump, neither, 's a blucher oxford; I don't believe you've ever tried to sell a thing in your life. Go on, roll your hoop, you're worse than useless to me! [*As he moves slowly toward the door,* MYRA *says softly:*] Sure you're not hungry? You're walking kind of unsteady.

VAL: What's that to you? I've got dog's eyes—you don't like me!

MYRA: I didn't say that.

VAL: I can't read shoe sizes. I don't know suede from kid. You can't use me; I'm worse than useless! What does it matter whether I'm hungry or not? [*He shakes with fury.*]

MYRA [*very softly, gently, with a slight mournful, tender shake of her head*]: Lawd, child, come back in the mawning and I'll give you a job. [*She moves slowly over to the candles and blows them out.* VAL *stares at her dumbly.*]

VAL: God, I—! Lady, you—!

MYRA [*laughing a little*]: God you an' lady me, huh. I think you are kind of exaggerating a little in both cases. [*They laugh. She blows out more of the candles leaving two lighted.*] You never have any trouble getting to sleep?

VAL: No. I know how to relax.

MYRA: How do you relax?

VAL: Imagine yourself a loose piece of string.

MYRA: A loose piece of string. That's lovely! I'm a loose piece of string. [*There is a knock on the ceiling.*]

149

VAL: What's that knocking upstairs?

MYRA: Jabe. [*She averts her face.*]

VAL: Who?

MYRA: My husband.

VAL: It scared me for a minute.

MYRA: Why?

VAL: Clump. Clump. Clump. Sounds like a skeleton walking around upstairs.

MYRA: Maybe you're gifted with too much imagination. [*She bends over to blow out the last candle.*]

VAL: Uh-huh. That's always been one of my biggest troubles. [*The candles gutter out. A dog is heard baying in the distance; the sound has a peculiar, passionate clarity.*]

MYRA [*softly*]: Hear that houn' dawg? . . . He's bayin' at th' moon. . . . Sky's cleared off? . . . Yes, it's clean as a whistle. . . . Isn't that nice?

VAL [*hoarsely*]: Yes, Ma'am.

MYRA: Well. . . . [*It grows rapidly darker as they stand hesitantly apart, looking at each other.* MYRA *turns slowly back toward the stairs.*] Well . . . the door locks itself when you slam it. Good night.

VAL [*speaking in a low, hoarse whisper*]: G'night. [*She starts up the stairs, slowly. He opens the door. Once more the dog is heard baying. They both stop short as though caught by the magic of the sound and face each other again from the stairway and the door.* VAL *speaks again, still more hoarsely.*] G'night.

MYRA [*in a whisper*]: Good night.

CURTAIN

ACT TWO

It is about a week later. VAL *is seated on the counter of the store leaning dreamily against a shelf. In his hand is a pencil and a shoebox lid. He is raptly composing an idyllic passage in his book. The juke box is playing as he speaks aloud.* MYRA *appears in the confectionery archway with a couple of boxes. She overhears his soliloquy and stops short to listen.*

VAL: Day used to come up slow through the long white curtains.

MYRA: Val! [VAL *starts.*] Who are you talking to?

VAL: Myself, I suppose.

MYRA: Isn't that kind of peculiar, talking to yourself?

VAL: No, ma'am. That's just a habit that lonesome people get into.

MYRA: Please don't do it when anyone's in the store. I don't want it spread around town that a lunatic's been employed here. That sunshine's *terrific*—you better let down the awnings. [VAL *moves slowly from the counter.*] Slew-foot!

VAL: Huh?

MYRA: Slew-foot, slew-foot! You walk like you're on flypapers! Pick up your feet when you walk and get a *move* on! [VAL *laughs and saunters leisurely out the door.*] Talks to himself, writing poems on shoeboxes! What a mess. [*She stares through the window as* VAL *lowers the awning. Three young girls follow* VAL *as he comes back in.*]

A GIRL: Hello!

VAL [*amiably*]: Hello there.

THE GIRL: Jane wants to look at some kickies.

SECOND GIRL [*giggling*]: No— you do.

THIRD GIRL: I'd like to try on some. Can you dance in kickies?

VAL: Sure you can dance in kickies. Sit down there. Let's measure your little foot.

THE GIRL [*beating her to the chair*]: Me first, me first.

VAL: Okay. First come, first serve. [*He pulls her shoe off. She giggles spasmodically.*]

VAL: Five and one half, Bennie. [*He goes to the shelf.*]

THE GIRL: Isn't he cute?

SECOND GIRL: Say, do you dance?

THIRD GIRL: Would you like to go out jooking?

MYRA: Val! I'll wait on these girls. You take these empty boxes out of here. [*As soon as* VAL *leaves, the girls giggle and run out of the store.* MYRA *looks very annoyed as* EVA TEMPLE *enters.*]

EVA: Mr. Xa-*vier?*

MYRA [*sharply*]: Our popular young shoe clerk is in the basement. What do you want?

EVA: A pair of bedroom slippers.

MYRA: Sit down and I'll show you some.

EVA: I'll wait till Mr. Xavier comes back upstairs. He seems to understand my feet so well. How's Cousin Jabe this mawning?

MYRA: Just the same.

EVA: Dear me. [VAL *reappears.*] Mr. Xa-*vier!*

VAL: How are you this mawning?

EVA: I seem to be comin' down with th' most abominable earache.

MYRA [*sympathetically*]: Aww! Let me give you a little laudanum faw it.

EVA: No, thanks. I put some in already. I think Birdie Wilson was partially responsible faw it.

VAL: Why? Is earache contagious?

EVA: No, but Birdie was singing right next to me at choir practice, which did it absolutely no good. [*She titters a little.*] What'm I sittin' here faw?

VAL: T' look at some shoes.

EVA: Aw. Well, I guess I might. Haven't you all noticed about Birdie? Her voice always cracks on that *Te Deum.* She can hit "A" pretty good but she always flats on "B." You'd think she'd have better sense than to even attempt to make "C" because it's completely out of her range, but I'll say this for Birdie, she's got the courage of her convictions.

VAL: These are the new wine shades.

EVA: Oh! Pretty! Yes, she goes right on up there and I'm telling you all, it's a perfect imitation of the Cannonball Express. [*She giggles.*] Oh, my goodness, these *pinch!*

VAL: Do they?

EVA: They certainly do. [*She giggles archly.*]

VAL: Well, let's try a David on that.

EVA: What's David?

VAL: Next size broader!

EVA: Oh, my goodness, no! There must be some mistake!

VAL [*climbing the shelf ladder*]: Don't you know what a broad foot's a sign of, Miss Temple? Imagination! And also of ...

EVA: Of *what?* [CASSANDRA WHITESIDE *enters the front door.*]

MYRA: Hello, Sandra!

SANDRA: Hello, Myra. I just drove home from New Awleuns fo' the Delta Planters' Cotillion. And do you know I neglected to bring a single decent pair of evenin' slippers back with me.

MYRA: Oh, honey, we don't keep evenin' slippers in stock, we don't get any calls fo' them here.

SANDRA [*noticing* VAL]: I didn't suppose you would.

MYRA: Oh, wait! Val, reach me down that old Queen Quality box up there! [DOLLY *and* BEULAH *enter.*]

BEULAH: Well, it is exasperating to have your table broke up at the very last . . . *Sandra!*

DOLLY: Sandra Whiteside! I thought you were gonna stay in New Awleuns till after Mardi Gras.

SANDRA: I just drove home for the Delta Planters' Cotillion.

MYRA [*wistfully*]: How is Mardi Gras this yeah?

SANDRA: As mahvelously mad as usual. If I were refawming the world I'd make it last forever.

MYRA: I went to it once a long, long time ago. I remembuh they danced in the streets.

SANDRA: They do ev'rything in the streets!

MYRA: I was just fourteen, I had on my first long dress an' a marcel wave an' some perfume called *Baiser d'Amour* that I bought at the Maison Blanche. Something wonderful happened.

SANDRA: What was it?

MYRA: A boy in a Pierrot suit.

SANDRA: How lovely! What did he do?

154

MYRA: Caught me around the waist, whirled me till I was dizzy—then kissed me and—*disappeared!*

SANDRA: Disappeared?

MYRA: Completely. In the crowd. The music stopped. I ran straight back to my room and lay on the bed an' stared an' stared at a big yellow spot on the ceiling.

SANDRA: Oh, my Lawd, how tragic.

MYRA: It *was.* [*She smiles.*] I still can feel it whenever the carnival's mentioned.

SANDRA: Your first heartbreak!

MYRA: Uh-huh. [*She laughs.*]

VAL [*bringing a shoebox*]: This one?

MYRA: *Yes, that's it.* [*To* SANDRA:] I hope you're not superstitious!

SANDRA [*lighting a cigarette*]: Why?

MYRA: Because this box contains some silver and white satin slippers that were intended for Rosemary Wildberger ...

DOLLY: Rosemary!

BEULAH: Wildberger!

MYRA: . . . To wear at her wedding exactly three years ago this Valentine's Day. [*She lifts one of the slippers.*] She had such a tiny foot.

BEULAH: Such a tiny, delicate girl. Rosemary ...

DOLLY: Wildberger!

SANDRA [*laughing lightly*]: Well, what happened? Did she fall dead at the altar?

BEULAH: Oh, no.

DOLLY: Worse than that!

155

BEULAH: Much worse. The man stood her up.

MYRA: Where did Rosemary go, does anyone know?

BEULAH: Some people say she went crazy an' some people say she went to Cincinnati to study voice.

SANDRA [*carelessly*]: Which was it?

EVA [*piping up resentfully, having been ignored*]: Neither. She went into Chinese missionary work.

DOLLY [*sarcastically*]: Trust Eva Temple to have complete information.

BEULAH: Oh, yes.

SANDRA: And these are the fabulous Rosemary's little silver and white wedding slippers. How lovely.

MYRA: I ordered 'em from St. Louis for her but, of course, I never had the heart to mention them to her parents after she disappeared. What size do you wear, honey?

SANDRA: Four, triple A.

MYRA: Gracious. These are four B. Val, see how they fit Miss Whiteside. [*She turns to* DOLLY.] Oh, Dolly, I wanted you to see this; soon as I unpacked it I had a vision of you! [*She removes an outlandish red dress with brass trimming from the racks; it looks like a bareback rider's outfit.*]

DOLLY [*rushing to it*]: Oh, my God, ain't it lovely! But you know, honey, I won't be able to wear anything one piece this spring.

MYRA: Really?

DOLLY: Oh, for the usual reason. Y'know there's absolutely no justice in nature. I mean the way she ties some women down while others can run hog wild. Look at Myra, for instance. Not one kid an' me turning out the seventh.

156

MYRA [*averting her face*]: Bring your measurements—I'll order you some maternity garments from Memphis.

DOLLY: Measurements? Fifteen square yards. How long'll it take?

MYRA: Probably two or three weeks. [DOLLY *shrieks and throws up her hands.*] Can't you wait that long?

DOLLY: I can, but my figure can't. [BLANCH TEMPLE *enters, and trips over the rubber mat at the door. She utters a shrill cry.*]

EVA [*jumping up*]: Blanch, that might have *thrown* you!

MYRA: Val, you must tack that down.

VAL: Get the nigger to do it.

BLANCH: My ankle is twisted. I can't even step on that foot.

EVA: Oh, my Lawd, she'll have to have it treated again. Cost us five or six dollars. I simply can't pay for these shoes.

MYRA: All right, you don't have to, Eva, we'll just call it square. Val! Wrap these up for Miss Temple. [*She turns to* SANDRA.] How did they fit? [VAL *picks up the shoes and goes to the cash register.*]

SANDRA: I couldn't wear them. Let me see a pair of plain white pumps.

MYRA: Surely.

DOLLY: We must be goin', Beulah, bye, bye, you all. [DOL-LY *and* BEULAH *go out.*]

BEULAH [*Her voice is heard off stage*]: I just been thinkin'. Lulu Belle don't play contract at all. She just plays auction.

MYRA: Hurry back! [*She gets some other shoes down; sits on the stool; opens the box for* SANDRA.]

157

BLANCH [*peeking among the valentines on the counter*]: Here's where she must've bought it 'cause here's another just like it.

VAL: What's that?

BLANCH: Somebody sent us a comic valentine. It wasn't funny at all, it was simply malicious. Old maids. There's no such thing as an old maid anymore.

EVA: No, they're bachelor girls.

VAL [*suppressing a smile*]: Here's your shoes, Miss Temple.

EVA: Oh, thanks, aw'fly. Miss DeQuincy was telling me you'd been to Yellowstone Park.

VAL: I've traveled all over, not only Yellowstone Park, but Yosemite, Gran' Canyon . . .

BLANCH: How marvelous. Why don't we get him to give us a little descriptive talk at our next auxiliary meeting?

EVA: Oh, would you do that, Mr. . . . .

VAL: Xavier.

EVA: Mr. Xavier. You won't fo'get the meeting?

BLANCH: It's Saturday at four-fifteen.

MYRA: Val couldn't take the time off. We're too rushed on Saturday afternoon.

EVA: Aw, what a shame. I meant to ask you, how's Cousin Jabe?

MYRA: No better.

EVA: Aw. What exactly resulted from the operation in Memphis?

BLANCH: Is it true that . . .

EVA: It was too late for surgical interference?

MYRA: Yes, it is true.

158

BLANCH: Goodness gracious.

EVA: They cut him open and sewed him right back up?

MYRA [*turning away in distaste*]: Excuse me.

BLANCH: Eva.

EVA: What did I say?

BLANCH: Goodbye, Mr. Xavier. [*They go out.*]

SANDRA: Aren't they delightful. The little white doves of the Lord. [*With a sidelong glance at* VAL.] Do you suppose I'll get like that if I remain a virgin?

MYRA: Well, I don't believe I'd worry about it, Sandra. [JABE *knocks overhead.*]

SANDRA: Ouuu! What's that noise?

MYRA: Jabe's knocking. [*Her face darkens.*]

SANDRA: Oh.

MYRA: I'll have to run up for a minute. [*She goes quickly upstairs.*]

SANDRA [*lighting a cigarette, with a quizzical look at* VAL]: I didn't come in here for evening slippers.

VAL: No. I figured you didn't.

SANDRA: I didn't come home for the Delta Planters' Cotillion. I came back here to see you. I haven't been able to get you off my mind. I woke up thinking about you last night in the Hotel Monteleone. I went downstairs to the bar at three o'clock in the morning. I thought I might forget if I got drunk. They must've poured my whiskey out of the wrong bottle, though. At half-past three I was on the highway, headed back to Two Rivers—seventy, eighty, ninety miles an hour—scared that you'd be gone before I got here. What do you think about that?

VAL: I think you'd better go back to the Mardi Gras.

SANDRA: You don't like me very much, do you?

VAL: I want to keep this job. Every place I've gone to it's been some woman I finally had to leave on account of.

SANDRA: I believe that. You're the center of much discussion in Two River County—among the women. That snake-skin jacket, those eyes; that special technique you use in fitting on shoes.

VAL: I don't use any special technique.

SANDRA: Maybe they just imagine that you do. I can understand why. You're beautiful, you're wild. I have a feeling we'll come together some night.

VAL: Yeah?

SANDRA [*rhapsodically*]: In the dark of the moon, beside a broken fence rail in some big rolling meadow. [VAL *turns away.*] We won't even say hello.

VAL: Let's quit this!

SANDRA: This what?

VAL: Double talk.

SANDRA: All right. [*She removes her dark glasses and arches her body in a provocative pose. She speaks childishly.*] Why did you slap me, Val?

VAL: Because.

SANDRA: Just because?

VAL: I didn't want to be interfered with by you. You think I've got a sign "Male at Stud" hung on me?

SANDRA: Yes, I think you have. Nobody could possibly make a mistake about it.

VAL: You made a mistake about it. I'm not in your class. I'm the kind of fellow you get to wash your car or chop the cotton. That night you drove me up to Cypress Hill, I wasn't nothing to you. It was like you had hired me to give you a little amusement.

SANDRA: That's what you thought? You were wrong about that. I felt a resemblance between us.

VAL: There's none that I know of, lady.

SANDRA: You must be blind. You—savage. And me— aristocrat. Both of us things whose license has been revoked in the civilized world. Both of us equally damned and for the same good reason. Because we both want freedom. Of course, I knew you were really better than me. A whole lot better. I'm rotten. Neurotic. Our blood's gone bad from too much interbreeding. They've set up the guillotine, not in the Place de Concorde, but here, inside our own bodies!

VAL: Double talk, smart double talk.

SANDRA: No. Look at my wrists. They're too thin. You could snap them like twigs. You can see through my skin. It's transparent like tissue paper. I'm lovely, aren't I? But I'm not any good. I wear dark glasses over my eyes because I've got secrets in them. Too much of something that makes me rather disgusting. Yes, you were right when you slapped me, Val. You should have killed me, before I kill myself. I will some day. I have an instinct for self-destruction. I'm running away from it all the time. Too fast. New Orleans, Vicksburg, Mobile. All over the God damn country with something after me every inch of the way! But the poison I've got in my blood isn't the kind that makes me fatal to kiss! Why don't you kiss me, Val? [VAL *moves away from her but she follows him.*] Scaredy cat! *Scaredy cat!* [VAL *catches his breath and starts to embrace her. She suddenly jabs him in the middle with her knee and bites his hand. She laughs wildly.*] There! There now! That's what I came back for! Nobody's ever

161

slapped me and gotten away with it, Snakeskin! Goodbye! [*She runs out the door.*]

VAL: God damn little bitch! [MYRA *appears on the stairway.*]

MYRA: What did she do?

VAL: She dared me to kiss her.

MYRA: Did you oblige her this time or did you slap her again?

VAL: I would've done it if she hadn't kicked me.

MYRA: Well, I'm glad that she kicked you. You can find some other place to do your carrying on.

VAL: I wasn't carrying on.

MYRA: You just admitted you would have if she'd let you. [*She goes to the shelves.*] Oh, lights of delirium, look where you put the kids!

VAL: You didn't say where to put them.

MYRA: In six days time I thought you might've caught on to where some things belong in this store.

VAL: Look here, if I was a mind reader, lady, I'd put up a tent on the commons and tell your fate by the stars at fifty cents a disaster!

MYRA: Disaster is right! I wish you'd use your noggin for something beside sweet looks at the women! Anybody with the brain of a newborn calf should know better'n to put a bunch of kids in here with—look at that, will you? [*She tosses a box furiously to the floor.*] Those Queen Quality evening slippers stuck in here, too. Why don't you fill up the rest of the space with cigar boxes and candy bars? Why do you wanta show so little imagination that you don't put nothing but shoes in the Shoe Department? You're writing a book? Surely you can think of some fancy new ideas like hanging dresses from the ceiling fans!

VAL: Look here, Myra.

MYRA: Since when am I Myra to you? My name is Mrs. Torrance!

VAL: You call me Val.

MYRA: That's different. I'm the employer here, you work in my store!

VAL: You mean I *worked* in your goddam store! [*He tears off his white clerk's jacket and flings it to the floor. There is a shocked silence.*]

MYRA: I was going to give you your notice tonight, anyhow.

VAL: You don't have to give it to me, I've already took it.

MYRA: Well, you can't walk out in the middle of the day like this.

VAL: Why not? I'm no help to you.

MYRA: I didn't say that . . .

VAL: Oh, no? Actions speak louder than words, Mrs. Torrance! [MYRA *looks at him, stunned, as he puts on his snakeskin jacket. A Negro huckster passes along the street singing his wares.*] You are a very difficult, hardheaded woman—and much as I wanted a job I got to admit that working for you is no pleasure. When you tell me to do things, how can I understand you, the way you talk?

MYRA: The way I talk?

VAL: You talk to the *wall*. You talk to the *ceiling*. You never talk straight to *me!* You never even look in my face when you say something to me! I just have to guess what you

163

said 'cause you talk so fast an' hard an' keep your face turned away . . . I've had the feeling ever since I come here that everything I do has displeased you!

MYRA [*averting her face*]: I didn't mean to give you that impression. As a matter of fact I was pretty well satisfied with the way you were coming along.

VAL: You certainly kept your satisfaction a secret.

MYRA: I know, I know. I'm nervous, I'm cross, I'm jumpy. [*pathetically*] I thought that you understood my nervous condition and made some allowance for it!

VAL: Being nervous is no excuse for acting like a nine-tailed catawampus!

MYRA: What is a nine-tailed catawampus?

VAL: I don't know. But I sure would hate to meet one.

MYRA [*she is hurt*]: Oh! [*She raises a handkerchief to her eyes.*] How should I act with you—you carrying on with people like Sandra Whiteside—right here in the store!

VAL: So that's why you flew off the handle.

MYRA: Not just that. You know why those high school girls keep flocking in here?

VAL: Sure. To buy spring shoes.

MYRA: Spring shoes nothing! They come in here for a *thrill!*

VAL: A *what?*

MYRA: A *thrill.* You know what that is, don't you?

VAL [*laughing*]: Can I help it?

MYRA: Yes! You don't have to *give* them one.

VAL: How do I give them a thrill?

MYRA: Don't ask *me* how. You don't have to manipulate their knees to get shoes on them.

VAL: Manipulate their . . . I never *touch* their knees!

MYRA: I've got eyes in my head!

HUCKSTER [*chanting out in the street*]: Ahhhh ahhhh. Turnip greens, new potatoes, rutibagas. Ahhh-ahhh. Carrots, string beans, onions!

MYRA: Also your attitude is very suggestive.

VAL: Suggestive of what, Mrs. Torrance?

MYRA: Bedrooms, if you want to know.

VAL: Bedrooms!

MYRA: Yes!

VAL: That sure is peculiar. How do I do *that?*

MYRA: Everything that you do. The way you talk, the way you walk, every single motion of you. Slew-footing this way and that way like one of those awful, disgustin', carnival dancers! [*The huckster is heard calling further away.* VAL *stares at* MYRA *with a long troubled look.*]

MYRA: Quit looking at me like that! [*She sobs.*] I know how awful I look.

VAL [*gently*]: You don't look awful, Myra.

MYRA: Yes, I do—my hair all stringing down—my face always turns so red when I get worked up. [*She sobs and turns away.*]

VAL [*very gently*]: Myra—I mean, Mrs. Torrance. I wanted to keep this job. I was tired of moving around and being lonesome and only meeting with strangers. I wanted to feel like I belonged somewhere and lived like regular people. Instead of like a fox that's chased by hounds!

165

MYRA: Maybe I haven't understood you exactly.

VAL: No. You haven't.

MYRA: How could I though? You're still a stranger to me.

VAL: My name is Val Xavier.

MYRA: And mine is Myra Torrance. Now do you feel like you know me any better?

VAL: No.

MYRA [*still sobbing a little*]: Well, I don't feel much better acquainted with *you*. Give me one of them tissue paper things. [*She blows her nose.*]

VAL: How do you get to know people? I used to think you did it by touching them with your hands. But later I found out that only made you more of a stranger than ever. Now I know that *nobody* ever gets to *know* anybody.

MYRA: Nobody ever gets to *know* anybody?

VAL: No. Don't you see how it is? We're all of us locked up tight inside our own bodies. Sentenced—you might say— to solitary confinement inside our own skins.

MYRA [*giving him a long, puzzled look*]: Is that something out of The Book?

VAL [*grinning*]: No. That goes into The Book.

MYRA: You're a queer one. A lot of people have dropped in off the road since I've been here, but nobody quite like you. I can't figure out what you *belong* to, exactly.

VAL: Me? Belong to? Nothing.

MYRA: Don't you have folks anywhere?

VAL: I used to.

MYRA: What become of them?

VAL: I lost track of 'em after they lost their land.

MYRA: They worked on shares?

VAL: No, not shares—but leavings, scraps, tidbits! They never owned a single inch of the earth, but all their lives they gave to working on it. The land got poor, it wouldn't produce no more, and so my folks were thrown off it.

MYRA: Where did they go?

VAL: I don't know where. They were loose chicken feathers blown around by the wind.

MYRA: You didn't go with 'em?

VAL: No. No, I made up my mind about something and I've stuck to it ever since.

MYRA: What's that?

VAL: To live by myself. So when the others left, I stayed on Witches' Bayou. It was a good place to hide in. Big cypress trees all covered with long gray moss the sun couldn't hardly shine through. Not in chinks, though, not in squares but all spread out . . .

MYRA: Misty-like.

VAL: Yeah.

MYRA: How old were you? How did you live?

VAL: Fourteen. I lived like a fox. I hunted and fished but most of the time I was hungry. I guess it must've made me a little lightheaded, because I know I had some peculiar notions . . . I used to lay out naked in a flatboat with the sun on me.

MYRA: What did you do that for?

VAL: I had a feeling that something *important* was going to come *in* to me.

167

MYRA: In? Through your skin?

VAL: Kind of. Most people don't expect nothing important to come *in* to them. They just expect to get up early—plow—rest—go turtle-eggin' an' then back to bed. They never look up at the sky, dark—or with stars—or blazing yellow with sunlight—and ask it, "Why? why? why?"

MYRA: Did you ask it, "Why"?

VAL: That was the first word I learned to spell out at school. And I expected some answer. I felt there was something secret that I would find out and then it would all make sense.

MYRA: How would you find it out?

VAL: It would come *in* to me. Through my eyes—see? Through my ears, through my skin. Like a net—see? If you don't spread it out, you won't catch nothing in it. But if you do, you *might*. Mine I used to spread it out, wide-open, those afternoons on the bayous—ears pricked, eyes peeled—watchin', waitin', listenin' for it to come!

MYRA: Did it ever?

VAL: No. Never quite. It would of though, if I hadn't gotten thrown off the track by the girl.

MYRA: There was a girl. What girl?

VAL: A girl I met on the bayou.

MYRA: Oh, what about her?

VAL: She was the first one, yeah. That day I was real excited. I had a feeling that if I just kept polin' on a little bit further I'd come bang on whatever it was I was after!

MYRA: And she was it?

VAL [*violently*]: Naw, she *wasn't*. But she made me *think* she was.

MYRA: How did she do that?

VAL: How? By standin' naked on the dogtrot, in the door of the cabin, without a stitch on.

MYRA: What was she like?

VAL: J'ya ever notice the inside of a shell? How white that is?

MYRA: She was young I suppose. Very young?

VAL: Her shape up here, it wasn't no bigger than this [*slightly cupping his palm*]. I hadn't noticed before the special diff'rence in women.

MYRA: But you did then?

VAL: Yes, I did then.

MYRA: Was she . . . ?

VAL: What?

MYRA: More attractive than—anyone since?

VAL: She was—th' first.

MYRA: What did you do? What happened?

VAL: I poled th' boat up closer. An' she came out on the dogtrot an' stood there a while with the daylight burnin' around her as bright as heaven as far as I could see! Oh, God, I remember a bird flown out of the moss and its wings made a shadow on her! [*He bows his head.*] An' then it sang a single high clear note. An' as though she was waitin' for that as a kind of a signal—to *trap* me— she turned and smiled an' walked on back in the cabin!

MYRA: And you followed, of course? What was it like inside?

VAL: Inside it was—empty inside.

MYRA: It couldn't have been!

VAL: Well, maybe it wasn't, but all I remember's the bed.

MYRA: Only the bed?

VAL: Made out of cypress an' covered with heaps of moss.

MYRA: Doesn't sound nice.

VAL: Well, it was. She'd been lonesome.

MYRA: How did you know? Did she tell you?

VAL: She didn't have to. She had it carved in her body.

MYRA: Carved? Is lonesomeness carved in people's bodies? [*She unconsciously touches her own.*]

VAL: Kind of. Anyhow you can see it.

MYRA: Could you see it in anybody's?

VAL: Sure. You could see it. Or feel it.

MYRA [*softly*]: What did she say to you?

VAL: She couldn't talk much except in some cajun language. I taught her some words.

MYRA: Such as what?

VAL: Such as *love*.

MYRA: You taught her that?

VAL: It was then I thought I discovered what it was that I'd been hankerin' after all those times I used to go off on the bayou.

MYRA: You thought it was that? [*She turns to the shelves.*] You mean she answered "me"?

VAL: Her! Me! Us together! Then afterwards—afterwards I thought that wasn't it. I couldn't make up my mind. When I was with her, I quit thinking because I was satisfied with just that; that sweetness between us, them long afternoons on the moss. But when I'd left her, the satisfaction would leave me an' I'd be . . . like this. [*He clenches his fist.*] Right on the edge of something tremendous. It wasn't her. She was just a woman, not even a woman quite, and what I wanted was . . .

MYRA: Was *what?*

VAL: Christ, I don't know. I gotta find out!

MYRA: I guess your love for her didn't amount to so much after all. What did you do after that?

VAL: I made some money cane-grindin', sold a bunch of 'gator an' diamondback skins. And bought myself a jalopy. I took to moving around. I thought I might track it down, whatever it was I was after. It always kept one jump ahead of me. That went on for ten years. Then I settled down for a spell in Texas. Seemed like the restlessness had worn off and I might get connected with something. But things went wrong. Something happened.

MYRA: What?

VAL: Never mind what. But everything was different after that. I wasn't free anymore. I was followed by something I couldn't get off my mind. Till I came here . . .

MYRA: Well, now that you've come here and got a good job, you can live a regular life and forget all of that.

VAL: I don't forget as easy as you, Mrs. Torrance. You don't even remember that I've lost my job.

MYRA: You haven't lost your job.

VAL: I'm not fired, huh?

MYRA [*smiling and shaking her head*]: We both got a little upset but that's over.

VAL: God, I . . .

MYRA: God you and lady me? [*She laughs.*] What is this place, a funeral parlor? Let's have some lights, some music. Put something on the victrola.

171

VAL: What would you like?

MYRA: I like that Hawaiian number with the steel guitars.

VAL: Yeah, that one! [*He crosses to the confectionery and starts the music; then he comes back.*] Myra, you know the earth turns.

MYRA: Yes.

VAL: It's turning that way. East. And if a man turned west, no matter how fast, he'd still be going the other way, really, because the earth turns so much faster. It's no use to struggle, to try to move against it. You go the way the earth pulls you whether you want to or not. I don't want to touch you, Myra.

MYRA: No, I don't want you to.

VAL: It wouldn't be right for me to.

MYRA [*half questioning*]: On account of Jabe?

VAL: No, on account of you. You been good to me. I don't want nothing to hurt you. Let's shake hands with each other, huh?

MYRA: That's not necessary! [*Without knowing why, she is suddenly angry. She crosses to the foot of the stairs.*] Take off that horrible jacket and get back to work. I have to fix Jabe's lunch. [*He follows her to the stairs.*]

VAL: Why wouldn't you shake hands with me? You're not still afraid of me, are you? [MYRA *starts quickly upstairs.*] Mrs. Torrance! Myra! [MYRA *pauses a moment on the landing, looking down at him with nervous hesitation.*]

VAL [*in an intense whisper*]: Myra! [*She disappears through the door and slams it shut.* VAL *stares in bewilderment.*]

SLOW CURTAIN

SCENE TWO

It is several hours later on the same day. The mellow afternoon sunlight is muted. There is the puff-puff of the cotton gin. VAL *stands in the confectionery archway with his back to the audience. He is staring intently up at a large Coca-Cola ad through the arch. In conjunction with the beverage, this ad forcefully expounds the charms of a "Petty Girl" in a one-piece lemon-yellow bathing suit. She and* VAL *appear to be experiencing a long and silent spiritual communion. In his hand* VAL *has a coke. Slowly, dreamily, he elevates the bottle to his mouth. Outside, at some distance, a rooster crows longingly at the sun. A man enters the front door in boots and riding breeches, bearing a shotgun. He coughs twice to divert* VAL'S *attention from the seductive picture.*

VAL [*turning*]: Sorry, I was dreaming. Beautiful afternoon, huh?

MAN: I'd like to see Mrs. Torrance.

VAL: She's gone upstairs with her husband. He's not so well.

MAN: Tell her that David Anderson is here.

VAL: Just press that buzzer on the counter and she'll be down.

ANDERSON: Thank you. [*Hesitantly he follows this suggestion. The buzzer is heard above. After a moment, the door on the landing opens and* MYRA *appears. She descends a few steps. Then seeing* ANDERSON, *she stops short.*]

MYRA [*sharply, involuntarily*]: David! [*They exchange a long, wordless stare. Then* MYRA *recovers herself and comes down.*]

173

MYRA [*to* VAL]: Will you go to the drugstore for me?

VAL: What do you want?

MYRA: Nothing. I mean some ice cream.

VAL: A pint of vanilla? [MYRA *says nothing.* VAL *looks curiously at them both and goes out.*]

MYRA: Well.

DAVID: How are you, Myra?

MYRA: Very well, thanks. How are you?

DAVID [*staring at her*]: All right. [*There is an awkward pause.*]

MYRA: You came in here once before and I ordered you out.

DAVID: That was six years ago.

MYRA: No. Eight.

DAVID: Right after your marriage.

MYRA: Not so long after yours.

DAVID: You can't hold a grudge that long.

MYRA: Oh yes I can. I think I can hold one forever. What do you want?

DAVID: Cartridges.

MYRA: You're going out shooting wild birds? I don't have to wish you luck. I haven't forgotten what a good marksman you were. Here's your cartridges. Is there anything else?

DAVID: It seems odd to see you in here, like this.

MYRA: Waiting on trade? Does that seem *common* to you?

DAVID: No. You never were practical, though. You were always such a . . .

174

MYRA: *Fool? Yes!* But I've changed since then.

DAVID: You haven't changed in appearance.

MYRA: Some women are like green things. They're kept on ice. I guess I'm one of that kind. You've changed a good deal. I wouldn't have known you at all except for your walk. You still move around like you were the lord of creation. I should think you might have found out by this time that your ten thousand acres don't make up the whole universe. Other people have got some property, too. I have this store, for instance. I don't have to *clerk* in it either. I *have* a clerk. [*Her voice trembles.*] I haven't come down so terribly far in the world.

DAVID [*embarrassed*]: Of course you haven't.

MYRA: No, I've gone *up.* And I'm going to go up still *higher.*

DAVID: I'm glad of that, Myra. People have told me about your husband's sickness. I . . .

MYRA [*feverishly*]: Yes. He's dying. After his death I'm planning to sell the store. Thirty or thirty-five thousand it ought to be worth. I'm planning to leave Two River and travel around. Florida, California, New York. I've been an object for pity for a little too long around here. "Poor Myra, she's hopeless, she's crushed!" That isn't exactly the truth and I'm tired of having it whispered behind my back. My life isn't over, my life is only *commencing.* A dollar ten for the cartridges, please.

DAVID [*extending the money*]: Here, Myra.

MYRA: Just put it down on the counter. Now get out. Don't ever come back here again.

DAVID [*quietly*]: All right, Myra. [*He goes slowly out.* MYRA *looks after him. A rooster crows mournfully in the*

distance. MYRA *raises her hand to her lips. She looks stunned.*
VAL *enters. He grins at her.*]

VAL: Finished your talk?

MYRA [*vaguely*]: Yes, David.

VAL: David?

MYRA [*starting*]: Excuse me, I mean "Val." [*bitterly*] I
made a fool of myself.

VAL: Huh?

MYRA [*evasively*]: That rooster always crows about sun-
down. Sounds like he's remembering something. [JABE *knocks
on the ceiling.*] I wonder if he *is*. [*She goes back upstairs.*
VAL *opens the ice cream, dips it out with his fingers.* VEE
TALBOTT *enters, stops short in the doorway as though dazed.
The rooster crows.*]

VAL: Oh, hello, Mrs. Talbott.

VEE: Something's gone wrong with my eyes. I can't see
nothing.

VAL: Here, let me help you. You probably drove up here
with that setting sun in your face.

VEE: What? Yes. That must be it.

VAL: There now. Sit down right here.

VEE: Oh, thank you so much.

VAL: I haven't seen you since that night you let me sleep
in the lockup.

VEE: Has the minister called on you yet? Reverend Tooker?
I made him promise he would. I told him that you were new
in the community and that you weren't affiliated with any
church yet. I want you to visit ours.

VAL: Well, that's mighty gracious of you, Mrs. Talbott.

176

VEE: The Church of the Resurrection! Episcopal, you know. Some people, especially Catholics, think our church was founded by Henry the Eighth, that horrible, lecherous old man who had as many wives as a cat has lives! There's not a word of truth in it. We have direct Apostolic Succession through St. Paul, who converted the early Angles. Angles is what they called the original English.

VAL: Angles, huh?

VEE: Yes, Angles. Our church is sometimes known as the Anglican Church.

VAL: Well, now, that's right int'restin', Mrs. Talbott. What's that picture you got? Something to put on display?

VEE: I thought that Myra might put it up with the Easter decorations.

VAL: I tell you what. We'll put it on display in the confectionery. Myra is going to do it over for spring. What's this picture of?

VEE: The Church of the Resurrection!

VAL: I didn't recognize it.

VEE: Well, I give it a sort of imaginative treatment.

VAL: Aw. What's this?

VEE: The steeple.

VAL: Is the church steeple red?

VEE: Naw.

VAL: Why did you paint it red then?

VEE: I felt it that way. I always paint a thing the way that it strikes me instead of always the way that it actually is. That's why the New Awleuns artists took an in'rest in my work. They say that it shows a lot of imagination. Primitive

177

is what they call it an' one of my pictures they've hung on *ex*-hibition in the Audubon Park museum! [*Her voice shakes with pride as she states this.*]

VAL: Aw. [*He crouches slowly in front of her with a faint smile.*] You need some new shoes.

VEE: Do I?

VAL: Yes. I'll sell you a pair of beautiful wine-colored slippers. [*He clambers quickly up the ladder and jerks out a box.*]

VEE: I don't know.

VAL: Come on. Sit down there. Give me your foot. [*He grasps it roughly and jerks the shoe off. He clasps her foot in both hands and rubs it.*] You got a bad circulation.

VEE: What?

VAL: Your feet are cold. Know why? These here elastic garters are too tight on you. Why don't you leave 'em off and roll your stockings like the other girls do?

VEE: Uh?

VAL: Skittish?

VEE: It's late; I got to be going!

VAL: With one shoe off and one shoe on? "Hey diddle, diddle, my son Tom!" Here, I'll put it back on for you. Just lean on my shoulder a minute!

VEE: No, I . . . [*She sways precariously.*]

VAL: Watch out. [*He clutches her about the thighs and looks up at her, grinning.*] There now! Got your balance?

VEE [*catching her breath sharply*]: Oh, I got to be *going!*

VAL [*jumps away from her, clambers up the ladder and places the picture on the shelf*]: How's that, Mrs. Talbott? Okay? [VEE, *still too startled to speak, turns vaguely and barges out of the door.* VAL *looks after her, then suddenly breaks into lighthearted laughter.* MYRA *comes back downstairs slowly with a tense, concentrated expression.* VAL *smiles.*]

VAL: Myra, did you ever see a red church steeple?

MYRA [*absently*]: No.

VAL [*chuckling*]: Neither did I.

MYRA: Jabe's took a turn for the worse. I had to give him morphine.

VAL: So?

MYRA: He must be out of his mind; he says such awful things to me. Accuses me of wanting him to die.

VAL: Don't you?

MYRA: No! Death's terrible, Val. You're alive and everything's open and free, and you can go this way or that way, whichever direction you choose. And then all at once the doors start closing on you, the walls creep in, till finally there's just one way you can go—the dark way. Everything else is shut off.

VAL: Yes . . . [*then abruptly*] You got the sun at the back of your head. It brings the gold out in your hair!

MYRA [*diverted*]: Does it?

VAL: Yes, it looks pretty, Myra. [*They stand close together. She moves suddenly away with a slight, nervous smile.*]

MYRA: It's closing time.

VAL: Uh-huh. I'll put these back on the shelves. [*He picks up the wedding slippers.*] She had a small foot.

MYRA: Rosemary Wildberger?

VAL: Naw, naw, that Whiteside bitch.

MYRA: I could wear these slippers.

179

VAL: They'd be too small.

MYRA: You want to bet? Try them on me.

VAL [*laughing*]: Okay! [*He slips the shoes on her feet.*] Pinch, don't they?

MYRA: No, they feel marvelous on me!

VAL [*doubting*]: Aw!

MYRA: They do! [*She looks down at them.*] Silver and white. Why isn't everything made out of silver and white?

VAL: Wouldn't be practical, Myra.

MYRA: Practical? What's that? I never heard of practical before. I wasn't cut out for the mercantile business, Val.

VAL: What was you cut out for? [*A derelict Negro,* LOON, *stops outside the door and begins to play his guitar in the fading warmth of the afternoon sun. At first the music is uncertain and sad; then it lifts suddenly into a gay waltz.*] What *was* you cut out for, Myra?

MYRA [*enrapt with the music*]: Me cut out for? Silver and white! Music! Dancing! The orchard across from Moon Lake! You don't believe me, do you? Well, look at this. You know where I am? I'm on the Peabody Roof! I'm dancing to music! My dress is made out of *mousseline de soie!* Yes, with silver stars on it! And in my hair I've got lovely Cape jasmine blossoms! I'm whirling; I'm dancing faster and faster! A Hollywood talent scout, a Broadway producer: "Isn't she lovely!" Photographers taking my pictures for the *Commercial Appeal* and for the *Times-Picayune,* for all the society columns and for the rotogravure! I'm surrounded by people. Autograph seekers, they want me to sign my name! But I keep on laughing and dancing and scattering stars and lovely Cape jasmine blossoms! [*Her rhapsodic speech is suddenly interrupted by* JABE'S *furious knocking on the ceiling. Her*

elation is instantly crushed out. She stops dancing.] I thought
he had enough to go to sleep . . .

VAL: Why don't you give him enough to . . .?

MYRA: Val! I'm a decent woman.

VAL: What's decent? I never heard of that word. I've written a book full of words but I never used that one. Why?
Because it's disgusting. Decent is something that's scared like
a little white rabbit. I'll give you a better word, Myra.

MYRA: What word is that? [*The guitar changes back to its
original slow melody.*]

VAL: Love, Myra. The one I taught the little girl on the
bayou.

MYRA: That's an old one.

VAL: You've never heard it before.

MYRA: You're wrong about that, my dear. I heard it mentioned quite often the spring before I got married.

VAL: Who was it mentioned by—Jabe?

MYRA: No! By a boy named David.

VAL: Oh. David.

MYRA: We used to go every night to the orchard across
from Moon Lake. He used to say, "Love! Love! Love!" And
so did I, and both of us meant it, I thought. But he quit me
that summer for some aristocratic girl, a girl like Cassandra
Whiteside! I seen a picture of them dancing together on the
Peabody Roof in Memphis. Prominent planter's son and the
debutante daughter of. . . . Of course, after that, what I really
wanted was death. But Jabe was the next best thing. A man
who could take care of me, although there wasn't much talk
about love between us.

VAL: No. There was nothing but hate.

MYRA: No!

VAL: Nothing but hate. Like the cancer, you wish you could kill him.

MYRA: Don't! You scare me. Don't talk that way. [*She crosses slowly to the door and* LOON *sings as the scene dims out.*]

SCENE THREE

Immediately following, without a break in the music. LOON *stops playing, retreats inside the store, and* SHERIFF TALBOTT *follows.*

SHERIFF: Hey, Loon! Didn't I see you on Front Street this mawnin' an' tell you to clear out of town?

LOON [*entering store*]: I thought you was jokin', Cap'n.

SHERIFF: Well, you made a big mistake. We don't allow no unemployed white transients in this town an' I'll be dogged if I'm gonna put up with colored ones.

LOON: I ain't transient, Cap'n.

SHERIFF: Where you livin'?

LOON: Nowhere, right this minute. Slep' on the levee las' night.

SHERIFF: Where you workin'?

LOON: Nowhere, Cap'n. I'se dispossessed.

SHERIFF: Aw, you'se dispossessed! Where'd you pick up all that fancy langwidge? You mean that Mr. Henley got fed up with your no-'countness an' turned you offen his property?

LOON: He turned me off but not fo' no-'countness. I wukked *hard*.

SHERIFF: If you work hard, you oughta make the state a good road-hand. Come on, you're under arrest.

LOON: What fo', Cap'n?

SHERIFF: Vagrancy. Ten dollar fine or thirty days hard labor.

LOON: Cap'n Talbott, I likes nine-fifty of bein' able to pay that fine.

SHERIFF: Come along.

VAL: Just a minute. I owe this boy ten dollars on his guitar.

SHERIFF: Huh?

VAL: I just bought his musical instrument off him. Here's the money. [LOON *starts to turn it over to the* SHERIFF.] Just a minute. Put that in your pocket. You can't fine a man for vagrancy when he's got ten dollars, can you, Sheriff? Not if I'm acquainted with the law.

SHERIFF: Huh?

VAL: He's also got a job. Hey, Loon, you drop back in tonight an' give me a *lesson* on this thing. Okay?

LOON: Yes, suh! Okay! [*He shuffles hurriedly out. The* SHERIFF *stares hard and silently at* VAL. VAL *casually strums a chord on the guitar.* DEPUTY SHERIFF PEE WEE BLAND *wobbles ponderously into the doorway laughing heartily, having just delivered some witticism to the men on the porch. He notices the tension and beckons the others to enter. They have all been drinking.*]

MYRA [*re-entering; nervously*]: Val, take these boxes . . .

SHERIFF [*interrupting*]: Just a minute. [*He catches* VAL'S *arm as* VAL *starts to move past him.* VAL *jerks his arm free. All this happens very rapidly.*] You beat the county out of a good road-hand.

VAL: I thought he might be better as a musician.

SHERIFF: Musician, hell! That worthless no'count nigger?

VAL: A man's not worthless because he's dispossessed.

PEE WEE: Hear, hear! *Dispossessed!*

FIRST MAN: Where'd he pick up that Nawthun radical lingo?

SECOND MAN: Who's he talkin' about?

FIRST MAN: That nigger, Loon.

SECOND MAN: Come down here to organize our niggers?

FIRST MAN: Make them bosses, huh? Us chop their cotton for 'em?

PEE WEE: It's talk like that that's back of all our colored tenant trouble. [*He wobbles up to* VAL.] Dispossessed? Did you say *dispossessed?*

VAL: Yes, I *did.*

PEE WEE: How yuh figure a man can be dispossessed from somethin' that never was his'n.

VAL: The land belongs to the man that works the land!

PEE WEE: Hear, hear!

FIRST MAN: That's red talk!

SECOND MAN: Yeah, go back to Rooshuh!

FIRST MAN: Anybody don't like this guvement oughta go back to Rooshuh!

SECOND MAN: Pack 'em all off togethuh, Jews, and radicals, and niggers! Ship 'em all back to *Rooshuh!*

FIRST MAN: Back to Africa with 'em!

MYRA [*frightened*]: Sheriff, stop this disturbance! My husband is sick upstairs!

SHERIFF: Quiet down, you boys!

PEE WEE [*very drunk and sententious, he talks like a Southern orator of the old school*]: Yeh, you all hush up. I'm talkin' to this young fellow. Now, looky here: a nigger works on a white man's property, don't he? White man houses him an' feeds him an' pays him livin' wages as long as he *produces.*

185

But when he *don't,* it's like my daddy said, he's gotta be blasted out a th' ground like a *daid tree stump* befo' you can run a *plow* th'ough it! [*A third man enters; he is a huge lout.*]

THIRD MAN: What's this here?

FIRST MAN: Some red-neck peckerwood with a nawthun edjication's tellin' us how we oughta run our niggers!

MYRA: Sheriff, make them stop right now!

PEE WEE: That nigger, Loon, got dispossessed from nothin'. The land wasn't his.

VAL: No, nothin' was his. Nothin' but his own black skin and that was his damnation!

FIRST MAN: Listen to that!

SECOND MAN: The carpetbaggers are comin' back agin!

THIRD MAN [*going up to* VAL]: You know what I do when I see a snake?

VAL: No, what?

MYRA: Val!

THIRD MAN: I get me a good fork stick to pin it down with. Then I scotch it under the heel of my boot—I scotch its goddam yellow gizzards out!

SECOND MAN: Go *on!*

FIRST MAN: *Show* him, Pinkie.

MYRA: Sheriff! *Please!*

[*The* THIRD MAN *spits at* VAL'S *shoe.*]

VAL: You spit on my shoe! *Wipe it off!* [*He spits again.* VAL *knocks him down. The men close in about* VAL *like a pack of hounds. There is a near riot for a few moments. Then the* SHERIFF *disperses them.*]

186

SHERIFF: Come on, you all! Clear out! *Clear* out! Pee Wee, you're Deputy. Git these men out of here! [*The men are shoved out, grumbling.*]

MYRA: Those drunken stave-mill workers make nothing but trouble!

SHERIFF [*to* VAL]: Who are you? What's your name?

VAL: Val Xavier.

MYRA: Val didn't mean anything; he's just a talker.

SHERIFF: Where do you come from?

VAL: Any number of places! [*He picks up the guitar again.*]

MYRA: Down state—Witches' Bayou.

SHERIFF: Let him answer for himself, Mizz Torrance.

MYRA: Well, don't snap questions at him like he was up on trial. I know everything about this boy.

SHERIFF: You do, huh?

MYRA: Yes, I do. He come to me with the highest recommendations.

SHERIFF: Who from?

MYRA: Friends, relatives. He likes to talk. He's done some writing, but he's no more a radical than you or me! I give you my trusted word on it.

SHERIFF: It ain't a question of doubtin' your word, Mizz Torrance.

MYRA: All right. Goodbye. I'm closin' up the store.

SHERIFF: Just one more question, please. What's your draft number, buddy? [VAL *stares at him and strikes a chord on the guitar.*] *What's your draft number?*

187

MYRA [*quickly*]: Eight thousand an' something. Val, take those empty shoeboxes out to the incinerator! [VAL *goes out with the boxes.*]

SHERIFF: How do you happen to know his draft number?

MYRA: He happened to tell me this mawning. Is there anything else that I can do for you, Sheriff?

SHERIFF: Yes, ma'am. You can do yourself a favor an' get a new clerk. That impudent young peckerwood won't bring yuh nothin' but trouble. G'night. [*The* SHERIFF *goes out.* MYRA *leans exhaustedly against the door.* VAL *re-enters slowly.*]

MYRA: Oh, Val, Val, Val, why didn't you keep your head? Why didn't you hold your tongue?

VAL: A man has got to stick up for his own kind of people.

MYRA: Your kind of people? That old colored beggar, Loon?

VAL: We're both of us dispossessed. Just give me my wages an' I'll be moving along.

MYRA: Where?

VAL: Where I was headed when I broke that axle. [MYRA *stares at him speechlessly.*]

MYRA: Val, I don't want you to go.

VAL: I'd ruin your business for you.

MYRA: Never mind that.

VAL: Besides I'm under suspicion now, and it wouldn't be safe.

MYRA: Just wait. This'll all blow over.

VAL: No. There's something I didn't mention about me this mawning.

188

MYRA: What happened in Texas?

VAL: Yes. I'm *wanted*, Myra.

MYRA: Wanted? You're *wanted?* [VAL *gravely picks up the guitar, without looking at* MYRA, *and strikes a slow chord on it.*] What are you *wanted* for, Val?

VAL [*quietly, without looking up*]: For rape.

MYRA: What?

VAL: Rape!

MYRA: Shhh! I don't believe it. That's something *nigguhs* are lynched for—not *you,* Val.

VAL: Yes, me. [*He strikes a chord on the guitar.*]

MYRA: When did it happen?

VAL: About two years ago.

MYRA: Who was the woman? [VAL *punctuates his speech with strumming on the guitar which he never puts down till the end of the scene. He avoids* MYRA'S *eyes.*]

VAL: A woman from Waco, Texas. Wife of an oil-field superintendent. I boarded with them while I was working down there. A plain sort of woman; I never noticed her much. One night her husband got drunk. Passed out in the car. This woman from Waco come to my room that night. Well, I was drunk. What happened was accidental. Afterwards, I was disgusted with her and with me, I said to her, "Listen, I don't want nothing like this; I'm getting away!" "I'm goin' with yuh," she said. "Oh, no you're not," I told her, "I travel alone." She started to scream. She run to the phone and screamed that she'd been raped. I lost my head for a minute and struck her in the mouth. Then I left. I drove clean out of Texas before daybreak. But not long

189

afterwards, though, I begun to see my name and my description in public buildings—"Wanted for Rape in Texas."

MYRA: You've changed your name.

VAL: Yes, but not my description.

MYRA: That's why you're quitting this job. You're scared she'll track you down?

VAL: Not just for that reason. I have another reason.

MYRA: What's that?

VAL: *You*. Like I told you this morning, I oughtn't to touch you, but I keep *wanting* to, Myra.

MYRA: Oh.

VAL: You don't get rid of something by holding it in. It gathers, it grows, it gets to be *enormous*.

MYRA: Yes.

VAL: You said this morning I touched the women too much when I tried shoes on them. Maybe I do. My hands—I'm afraid of my hands. I hold them in so hard the muscles ache. [*He strikes a chord sharply*.] You know what it's like? A herd of elephants, straining at a rope. How do I know the rope won't break sometime? With you or with somebody else?

MYRA [*going slowly to the door*]: You don't have to leave on account of a reason like that. [*She touches her forehead.*] My head's still whirling from all that excitement in here. I don't seem able to *think*. The cotton gin bothers me, too. It makes a sound like your heart was pounding a lot too fast.

VAL: Mine does sometimes. [*Strumming*.]

MYRA: Everyone's does sometimes.

VAL: Your belt's untied in the back.

MYRA: Is it? Fix it for me.

190

VAL [*slowly he sets down the guitar on the counter; crossing slowly to her, he touches her waist*]: You come way in at the middle.

MYRA: I haven't let go of my figure like some women do. I've kept it.

VAL: For what?

MYRA: What for? Maybe because I don't feel everything's done for me yet.

VAL: Why should you?

MYRA: Some women do about my age. They have babies.

VAL: You never?

MYRA: No. I lived in a state of—what do they call it?—artificial respiration. Something that pumps the breath in and out of your body when otherwise you'd be dead. Dead as a rock is, Val! [*She turns abruptly to him.*] Oh, Val, I don't want you to go. I'll make it all right. I'll fix things up so nobody's going to suspicion. I'll make up all kinds of stories if you'll stay here! Huh? Huh, Val?

VAL [*hoarsely*]: Myra. . . .

MYRA: Yes?

VAL: Let's—let's—go in the back room a minute. [*The cotton gin can be heard in the distance.*]

MYRA: That room's locked, Val.

VAL: Where's the key?

MYRA: I took it an' thrown it away.

VAL: What did you do that for?

MYRA: Because I known you would ask me to go in there sometime an' I was scared I might be weak enough to do it. So I took the key and I thrown it away so far I don't think

191

you could find it. [*He releases her and goes quickly out through the confectionery. The gin seems to pump even louder. After a moment Val returns to the room.*]

VAL [*in a hoarse whisper*]: That lock was no good, Myra.

MYRA: You broke it open?

VAL: Yes.

MYRA: Christ! I was scared that you would. [*For a long moment they stare at each other, then rush together in a convulsive embrace.*]

CURTAIN

ACT THREE

SCENE: *The same, but the room in the rear through the arch has been redecorated. The walls have been painted pale blue and have been copiously hung with imitation dogwood blossoms to achieve a striking effect of an orchard in full bloom. The room is almost subjective, a mood or a haunting memory beyond the drab actuality of the drygoods department. Its lighting fixtures have been covered with Japanese lanterns so that, when lighted, they give the room a soft, rosy glow. It is a rainy spring afternoon about two months after the preceding scene. The old-fashioned lights of the store cannot entirely dispel the silvery gloom. The Gothic features of the room are accentuated by this shadowy effect.* VAL *is alone in the store. He is working on his book, the loose pages of which he keeps in a battered old tin box. He writes with a stub pencil which he chews reflectively; then scribbles with rapt expression. The juke box is playing a number with steel guitars. He looks very simple and lonely, a little faunlike, seated on one of the low shoe-fitting stools, absorbed in his creative labor. There is a faint whisper of rain, and of wind.* MYRA *enters from the street in a transparent white raincoat, very glowing and warm and happy.* VAL *quickly stuffs the script back in the box and pushes it out of sight.*

MYRA: Hello, hello, hello! What are you hiding from me? Is it the book? Ah, the mysterious book. I never was quite sure that it existed.

VAL: What d'ja think it was?

MYRA: Something you dreamed those afternoons on the bayou! Let me look at it.

VAL: No.

MYRA: Let me just hold it.

193

VAL: Don't be silly.

MYRA: Please! [*He surrenders the bundle of papers grudgingly.*] It's like holding a baby! Such a big book, too; so good an' solid.

VAL: It's got life in it, Myra. When people read it, they're going to be frightened. They'll say it's crazy because it tells the truth! Now, give it back to me, Myra. It's not finished yet.

MYRA: I wish that I had something to do with it, too. Wouldn't it make it kind of more legitimate like if it had two parents, Val? [*She laughs tenderly, and hands it back to him.*] I had a wonderful time this afternoon. After I got Jabe's new prescription, I drove over to Tunica to get my hair done. I knew it would be my last chance before Easter. How does it look, Val?

VAL: Swell.

MYRA: How're things going?

VAL: Slow. I haven't rung up a single cash-sale since noon.

MYRA: Rain, rain. You certainly kill our trade. I was stuck on th' road coming home for nearly an hour before I got pulled out. [*She takes off her raincape and puts on a bright smock.*] I kind of enjoyed it, though. The air was so fresh, an' when the bells started ringing ...

VAL: What're they ringing for?

MYRA: Good Friday church service. Dr. Hector is preaching the Seven Last Words from the Cross. Just as they started to ring, a big white moth flew in the car window. Val, I hate most bugs, but this one I felt a kind of a sympathy for. He was terribly young.

VAL: How do you know he was young? Did you ask him his age?

194

MYRA: No, but he had that surprised, inexperienced look about him that young things have. It was easy to see he had just come from the cocoon, and was *sooo* disappointed. Of cou'se he expected th' world t' be bright an' gold, but what he found was a nasty, cold spring rain. His two long whiskers were covered with strings of pearls. He sat on the steering wheel an' shook them off. I asked him, "Why?" An' he said, "Don'tcha know? It's in bad taste to put on pearls before dark!"

VAL: You're talking foolishness, Myra.

MYRA: Am I? Fo'give me, da'ling. I'm in that kind of a humor. My God, you got eyes that shine in th' dark like a dawg's. [*She starts humming a tune.*] Remember that? Such a long time ago. Before Columbus discovered America even. Oh, beautiful fo' spacious skies, for amber fields of grain. . . . Greta Garbo is at the Delta Brilliant. . . . Fo' purple mountain majesties, above the fruited. . . . Lemme up on that ladder. I want to be on a high, high place in the sun! What's these here?

VAL: Women's soft sole slippers. They just come in. [*Impulsively she gathers them up like an armful of plushy red flowers and tosses them into the air.*]

MYRA [*ecstatically*]: Wake me early, Mother, fo' I shall be Queen of the May!

VAL: For Chrissakes, Myra, what did'ja do that for?

MYRA: Oh, soft sole slippers. Women's soft sole slippers! They seem t' be so damned unnecessary!

VAL: What's the matter with you this afternoon?

MYRA: When people have dreams, unusually good dreams, they get up singing, they go to the beauty parlor, and act like fools all day! When serious-minded people who write big

195

books say, "What's th' matter with you?" they simply smile an' say, "We have our secrets." [VAL *opens the door.*] The rain's slacked up?

VAL: Yeah, a little.

MYRA: That's good. Maybe we'll have a nice bright Easter, Val. We'll go to church an' look so lovely the Lawd will have to fo'give us for all our sins!

VAL [*in the doorway*]: River's way up over flood-stage at Friar's Point Landing. They say sometimes this place is cut off by water.

MYRA: They say! They say! What of it? Ten thousand years from today we'll just be little telltale marks on the sides of rocks which people refer to as fossils. [*There is the sound of slow tolling bells across the wide, rainy fields.*] That's all will be left of our big tremendous adventures! [*She smiles with amazement at this thought.*] Teeny-weeny little pencil-scratches, things like pigeon tracks will be what's left of Myra—what's left of Val! Then old Mr. Important Scientific Professor will pick up his microscope—"Humph!" he'll say, "This girl had remarkable legs." Or, "Goodness, this young man lost a rib somewhere." That will be all they'll ever find out about us! Were we in love? Were we happy? Did white moths fly in our windows? How do they know? They can't tell. History isn't written about *little* people. All that little people ever get to be is marks on rocks called *fossils*.

VAL: Yes, unless they write books or something.

MYRA: Oh, yes, of course, unless they write books or something! Then they're remembered *always!* [*She jumps down from the ladder and hugs him tenderly against her.*] You will be, da'ling! Don't worry!

196

VAL: Sarcasm?

MYRA: No, not a bit! [*She laughs gently.*] You're such a wonderful, wonderful baby! When I'm a fossil, even if it makes Mr. Science Professor blush, I hope he discovers my scratches are all scrambled up with yours. [*She laughs gaily. A small* NEGRO BOY *enters the store.*] Wipe yo' feet off, sonny, don't track th' floor.

BOY: Yes, ma'am.

MYRA: What do you want? Peanuts?

BOY: I wan' peanuts, but granny wan' a nickel's worth a snuff.

MYRA: Aw. Well, Granny's got to have her snuff, now, don't she? How is Granny feelin'?

BOY: She been laid up in bed with breakbone fever.

MYRA: Aw, now, that's a shame. You tell 'er Mizz Torrance say to get well quick, quick, quick, cause we can't do without 'er. [*A young* NEGRO *enters in overalls.*]

BOY: Yes, ma'am.

NEGRO: Howdy, Mizz Torr'nce.

MYRA: Hello, Bennie. Val, give the little boy a bag full a goobers, will yuh? They're on th' house.

NEGRO [*admiringly*]: You sho' are gracious, ma'am. I wunder if you would take my note for somethin'?

MYRA: Bennie, I've got enough notes from you to paper th' store with already. What do you want?

NEGRO: A little plug tobacco.

MYRA: Well, put your cross on this.

197

NEGRO: Thanks, ma'am. [*The* NEGRO BOY *comes back out with the peanuts and goes out the front door. There is a sound of shouting.*]

MYRA: Oh, they're shouting up over there at the big Lent meeting. Sounds like they might be hitting the sawdust trail.

NEGRO: Will be before sundown.

MYRA: How 'bout you, Bennie?

NEGRO: Me hit it? Naw, I guess I glories too much in the flesh for that. Good afternoon, Mizz Torrance.

MYRA [*to the* NEGRO]: Good afternoon. Where you takin' that load of sandbags to?

NEGRO: Down river t' Mr. Sikeses.

MYRA: You think there's a chance the levee might go out?

NEGRO: Ah reckon not unless th' Lawd intends it to. G'by, ma'am.

MYRA: Goodbye. [*The* NEGRO *starts the mules. His wagon wheels are heard.*] Val? [*There is no answer. She switches on the lights in the confectionery. Spring blooms with a soft radiance for an instant and then dies out as she releases the switch.*] Val! [*She turns smiling slightly, her lips moving as she whispers, excitedly, to herself. With a sudden, rapturous awareness she draws her hands up the front of her body and clasps them over her breasts.*] Oh . . . [*In the archway there is suspended a string of Chinese glass pendants with a tiny gong. With an impulse of childish gaiety, she sets the pendants tinkling, softly, musically, in the store's greenish gloom and she laughs to herself with a child's quick, delicate laughter. While her back is turned, the* CONJURE MAN *glides noiselessly into the store. Now, for the first time, there is a low muttering of thunder. The lights in the confectionery flicker a little. Still unaware of the* CONJURE MAN'S *presence,* MYRA

198

shivers slightly and a bewildered, uncertain look appears on her face and she raises a hand to touch her cheek and her forehead. As though with a disturbing prescience of something unnatural, she turns about slowly and meets the NEGRO'S *gaze. She catches her breath in a sudden, sharp gasp. The* CONJURE MAN *smiles and makes a slight obeisance. He stretches out his small clawlike hand, in the hollow of which he is presenting some object.*]

MYRA [*breathlessly*]: What—what do you want? [*The* CONJURE MAN *mumbles something which cannot be heard.*] What? No! No, I don't want it. [*then, smiling defiantly*] I don't need holy stones to bring me luck. [*The* CONJURE MAN *makes another slight bow, then starts to turn away.*] If you want to make an honest dollar, though, you can go out back and wash the Mississippi Delta off my car. You'll find a sponge, a bucket, and a bunch of old chamois hanging in the garage. [*The* CONJURE MAN *mumbles some eager words of thanks and starts to enter the confectionery.* MYRA *looks after him, troubled, not knowing why. In the archway he stops and looks back over his shoulder to meet her gaze. There is a moment of curiously tense stillness. Then he grins and makes another slight bow and disappears. There is the sound of low thunder again. The front door opens and* DOLLY *comes in.*]

DOLLY: Has he gone?

MYRA: Who?

DOLLY: That *awful* lookin' ole darky.

MYRA: He's gone out back. Who is he?

DOLLY: They call him the Conjure Man—from Blue Mountain. When I first caught a sight of him out there, I swear to goodness I neahly had a conniption! I was scared

199

to death that he would *mark* my *baby!* Which reminds me to ask you! Have those maternity garments got here yet?

MYRA: No, they haven't come yet.

DOLLY: What? I ordered 'em two months ago.

MYRA: I know, and I can't understand what's causin' the delay.

DOLLY: Neither can I. My God, what am I going to do?

MYRA: I'm sorry.

DOLLY: I guess I'll have to hang out a sign, "Excuse me, people." [MYRA *turns away in distaste.* BEULAH *rushes in.*]

BEULAH: Excitement! Cassandra Whiteside's come in town drunk as a lord.

DOLLY: No.

BEULAH: I just seen her on Front Street. Wearin' a white satin evenin' dress. She's been in another wreck; the side of the car's bashed in.

DOLLY: I thought they revoked her license.

BEULAH: She's got her a nigger chauffeur. At least I *hope* he's a chauffeur.

DOLLY: Beulah.

BEULAH: Well, there has been a great deal of speculation about 'em that's not very pleasant. They say that she's been ostracized in Memphis, asked to leave sev'ral parties; and her father has actually received a warning note from the Klan.

DOLLY: Goodness. She'll be worse than ostracized if she keeps up at this rate.

BEULAH: Myra, what will you do if she comes in here and starts to make a disturbance?

200

MYRA [*shortly*]: Put her out.

BEULAH: You think you could? They say she fights like a tiger.

MYRA [*as* VAL *enters*]: I think Val would be able to handle her for me.

VAL [*setting the boxes down*]: What did you call me for, Myra?

MYRA [*confused*]: Call you? Oh, yes, I—I can't remember just now.

BEULAH: That sounds extremely suspicious. [*She winks.*]

DOLLY: Don't it, though? Look, they're blushing.

BEULAH: Both of them. Oh, I think it's marvelous to see a man who can blush.

MYRA [*with nervous haste*]: Val, are those the new Keds?

VAL: No, women's rubbers.

MYRA: Just in time for the rain; how very lucky.

DOLLY [*meaningfully*]: How's Jabe?

MYRA [*still confused*]: Jabe?

DOLLY: Yes, your husband, honey. Jabe Torrance.

MYRA: Jabe's no better.

DOLLY: Ain't that turr'ble!

BEULAH: I don't guess you *could* look for much improvement.

MYRA: No. All we can do is try to relieve the pain. Val, bring up the rest of those boxes and stack them up there. [VAL *is glad to get out.*]

DOLLY: Myra, that green is your color!

BEULAH: Don't it look sweet on her, though? I had my eye on that dress; it's the nices' thing you had in stock, Myra Torrance.

MYRA: It's more of a blue than a green.

BEULAH: What do they call it?

MYRA [*with a slight, suppressed smile*]: They call it "ecstasy blue."

DOLLY: I swan. [*She exchanges a significant look with* BEULAH.]

BEULAH: But don't it become her, though? It brings the gold out in her hair.

DOLLY: *It does.*

MYRA: I just had it washed. That always brightens the color.

DOLLY: What with? Goldenfoam?

MYRA: No, with a few drops of lemon. That's all I use.

DOLLY: Honestly? Well, she's took on more *sparkle* this spring.

BEULAH: I think it's wonderful that you can be so brave.

MYRA: What do you mean?

BEULAH: Why, I mean about Jabe's condition.

MYRA: Oh, excuse me a minute. I gotta take Jabe his medicine. He's been so restless today. [*She goes back upstairs.* BEULAH *looks at* DOLLY *and giggles.* DOLLY *looks at* BEULAH *and giggles an octave higher. They both cover their mouths as the* TEMPLE SISTERS *enter.*]

BLANCH: I want you to know . . .

EVA: Dr. Hector had just finished preaching the Seven Last Words from the Cross . . .

BLANCH: When who should we run into . . .

EVA: Yes! on Front Street.

BEULAH: Sandra Whiteside?

EVA and BLANCH: Yes!

DOLLY: I know. We just been talking.

EVA [*catching her breath*]: Did you know she was just put out of the Cross Roads Inn?

BLANCH: Literally thrown out. They tried to get her father on the phone. Useless!

EVA: He's drunker than she is. We passed her just now up there on the Sunflower Bridge. She seemed to be having d.t.'s. What's that she was shouting, Blanch?

BLANCH: "Behold Cassandra! Shouting doom at the gates!"

EVA: Yes. An' some bright-skin nigger was in the car with her. It's really created a perfeckly terrible stir.

BLANCH: Imagine—on Good Friday!

EVA: Utterly shameless! Where's that nice-lookin' young man?

BLANCH: I got to return those shoes. I went to a very expensive obstetrician in Memphis. He said they'd ruined my feet. Why, Palm Sunday mawning I couldn't hardly march in church with the choir. [*She calls out.*] Mr. Xavier? Oh, they've closed the confectionery.

EVA: Yes. The noise was disturbing to Jabe.

BLANCH: She's had it redecorated.

EVA: All done over. She says it's supposed to resemble the orchard across from Moon Lake. [VEE *enters. She wears black, nunlike garments for Good Friday, and her look is exalted.*] Vee! How are you, honey?

203

VEE [*almost sobbing*]: I've waited and prayed so long. Now it's finally come.

BEULAH: *What's* come?

VEE: The vision. I seen him early this mawning. I painted the picture.

BEULAH: Picture of what?

VEE: Of Jesus!

DOLLY: I thought you said you'd never paint the Lawd until you'd actually seen Him face to face.

VEE [*simply*]: I have. This mawning. On the way to church, by the cottonwood tree, where the road branches off toward the levee. I been on a fast since Ash Wednesday to clear my sight. Veils seemed to drop off my eyes. Light— light! I never have seen such brilliance. Like needles it was in my eyes; they actually ached when I stepped out in it.

BEULAH: In what?

VEE: The sun this mawning, before the Passion began.

DOLLY: Weakness from fasting. You're such an excitable nature.

VEE: No, no. I've had other signs. Look at my palms.

BEULAH: What about them?

VEE: Can't you see the red marks?

BEULAH: They do look so't of inflamed.

BLANCH: Ain't that remarkable, though?

BEULAH: What happened?

VEE: I been tormented. He took all the torment off me.

DOLLY: Tormented by what?

204

VEE: Evil thoughts. Those men in the lockup, they write nasty words on the walls. At night I can see them. They keep coming up in my mind. He took that cross off me when he touched me.

BEULAH: Touched you?

DOLLY: Where? [VEE *lifts her hand reverently and touches her bosom.*] Aw. [*She giggles.*] He made a pass at you? [*She giggles.*] He made a pass at you?

BEULAH: Dolly, you're awful!

DOLLY: I couldn't help it; it just popped out of my mouth.

BEULAH: Vee, can't we see the picture?

BLANCH: Yes, let's *see* it.

VEE: I brung it here for Myra t' put on display. [*She starts to unwrap the canvas. There is the sound of an angry outburst and the simultaneous crash of glass on the floor above.*]

BEULAH: What's that? [*The women congregate quickly at the foot of the stairs in listening attitudes.*]

VEE [*at the right of* DOLLY]: No, I've had other manifestations. When I was seven years old, my little sister, Rose, got typhoid fever.

MYRA [*upstairs*]: Jabe.

BEULAH: What's that?

DOLLY: Can you make it out?

MYRA: Jabe!

BEULAH [*going to the foot of the steps*]: What's that shouting upstairs?

VEE: She hadn't been baptized yet an' the doctor said she was dyin'. So Reverend Dabney come over at midnight.

205

JABE: No, I won't take it.

MYRA: The doctor prescribed it for you. It helps the pain.

JABE: I know what you're trying to do. You're trying to kill me.

DOLLY: What?

BEULAH: What?

MYRA: You're out of your head.

DOLLY: What's that?

BLANCH: Sssh.

EVA: Sssh.

VEE: Afterwards, he give me the bowl of Holy water an' told me to empty it outside on the bare ground. But I didn't. I poured it out in the kitchen sink.

MYRA: Jabe, you don't know what you're saying. [*The door bangs open.*] I'll call for the doctor.

BLANCH: Delirious!

EVA: Yes, out of his haid!

VEE [*slowly*]: The kitchen sink turned *black. Black*—absolutely *black!* [*The door above is suddenly thrown open and* MYRA *calls out wildly.*]

MYRA: Val! Val!

DOLLY: I'll get him for yuh, Myra! Mr. Xavier. [*There is great excitement.* VAL *comes in.*]

VAL: What's the matter?

BLANCH: Oh, something's goin' on, I don't know what . . .

EVA: But it's awful! [MYRA *appears above.*]

MYRA: *Val?*

VAL: Yeah?

MYRA: Phone Dr. Bob, and tell him to come right over!
[*She slams the door.*]

EVA: Where's Dr. Bob?

BLANCH: Ain't he in Jackson Springs?

VAL: Howdy, Mizz Talbott.

EVA: I'm very much afraid the wires are down! [*As* VAL
crosses in front of VEE, *she slowly rises, following him with
her eyes, her lower jaw sagging open slowly with a stricken
expression.*]

VAL [*lifting the phone*]: Get me Jackson Springs. [VEE
utters a stifled cry. VAL *is struck by her shocked gaze.*] What's
the matter, Mizz Talbott? [*into the phone*] Jackson Springs?

VEE: No, no!

DOLLY: What's the matter with Vee? She's white as goat's
milk.

BEULAH: Seems to me like she's tooken some kind of a
spell.

DOLLY [*grasping her shoulders roughly*]: Vee!

VEE: Le' me go! Leave me be!

BLANCH: That vision she had has probably got her wrought
up.

EVA: Passion Week always upsets her. Get a wet cloth,
somebody!

VAL: The wires are down.

BEULAH: Don't Myra keep some kind of a stimulant on
the place?

VAL: There's some rum in the back. I'll get it.

VEE [*struggling up, panting*]: Naw, I can't stay, le' me go!

DOLLY: Nobody's holding you, honey.

VEE [*her eyes follow* VAL *as he crosses to the confectionery*]: Where's he going *to?*

BEULAH: Get you a little something to pull you together. [DOLLY *picks up the picture.*]

VEE [*crying out wildly*]: You take your hands off my picture! [*She wrests it from* DOLLY *before she can see it.*]

BEULAH: Well!

VEE: It's not t' be touched by you, you foul-minded thing!

DOLLY: I thought that you brung it here to put on display.

VEE: I never.

DOLLY: Just let me take one look!

VEE: No! [DOLLY *makes a move toward the canvas.* BEULAH *crosses to the right of the steps.* VEE *cries out and thrusts her away.* MYRA *appears on the stairs.*]

MYRA: Oh, for God's sake, will you all please hush up? I've got to get in touch with Dr. Bob! [*Her hair is disarranged, and her dress torn open as though she had been in a struggle.*] Jabe's delirious. He wouldn't take the morphine. Did you hear him? He said I was trying to kill him! [*She picks up the receiver, jiggles it.*]

EVA: Val tried to phone.

BLANCH: They told him the wires were down.

MYRA: Then I'll just have to drive over.

BLANCH: Oh, but they say there's danger of the bridge collapsing.

MYRA: What else can I do?

EVA: Blanch, if you were married and your husband was desperately ill, wouldn't you take a chance on the bridge collapsing?

BLANCH: No, I certainly wouldn't. No, I certainly. . . . Oh, before you go, Myra—about these shoes . . .

MYRA [*snatching a raincoat from the closet*]: Oh, I'm distracted, I—Val, tell the nigger to put the chains on the tires!

VAL: I can't do six things at once. Miss Eva here wants some money back on a pair of shoes.

MYRA: Money back? What money? You got the shoes for nothing!

BLANCH: Oh, horrors, don't you remember how I tripped over that rubber mat an' practickly broke my ankle?

EVA: Two trips to the doctor it cost us!

BLANCH: Six dollars!

EVA: But we'll take five since Myra has been so . . .

MYRA: Thanks. Val, give the ladies five dollars out of the cashbox. Now if you'll excuse me . . .

BEULAH: Myra, if there's anything I can do.

DOLLY: Don't hesitate to call on me if they is. [MYRA *has already disappeared through the confectionery.*]

BLANCH: Gracious . . .

EVA: Sakes alive! What excitement! Blanch, you go up an' sit with Cousin Jabe.

BLANCH: Oh, I couldn't. I'm having palpitations!

VEE: I . . . I . . . have to leave, too. [*She retreats toward the door.*]

209

DOLLY: Not without showin' the picture!

VEE: Dolly, get out of my way!

BEULAH [*snatches the picture held behind her back and tears the paper wrapping off; she gasps and shrieks with laughter*]: Mr. Xavier!

DOLLY: Mr. *Xavier?*

VAL: What?

BEULAH: Vee Talbott here has just conferred a wonderful honor on you.

DOLLY: Oh, so it *is*, I *suspected!*

BEULAH: You're going to sit at the head of the table with all of the Twelve Apostles sitting around'ja!

DOLLY: You even have a silver dishpan sort of on top of your haid. [*They both shriek with laughter.*]

VEE [*wildly*]: No, no, no! Let go of my picture!

BEULAH: Ain't it a wonderful likeness?

DOLLY: From memory, too. Or did you pose for it, Val?

BEULAH: He didn't *have to.* She seen him in the cotton-wood tree. The *lynching* tree, as they call it!

DOLLY: I hope that don't make you *nervous*, Val!

VEE: No! You're all of you cooking up something without no excuse!

DOLLY: No? No excuse? That's why you nearly collapsed when Mr. Xavier came up an' said hello to yuh!

BEULAH: Your spiritual nature an' all, what a big joke it is!

DOLLY: Carping at other people, criticizing their morals . . .

BEULAH: Stirring up all that card-playing rumpus here in the congregation.

DOLLY: Declaring in public that I wasn't fit to associate with because I had drinking parties.

BLANCH: Dolly!

EVA: Don't you all go on like this!

DOLLY: She's got to have her eyes opened, now, once an' for all. A vision of Jesus? No, but of Val Xavier, the shoe clerk who sold 'er them shoes.

VAL: Mrs. Bland!

DOLLY: And where did she have this vision? Where? Under the cottonwood tree where the road turns off toward the levee. Exactly where time an' time again you see couples parked in cars with all of the shades pulled down! And what did he do? He stretched out his hand and *touched* yuh! [*She thrusts her hand against* VEE'S *bosom.* VEE *cries aloud as though the hand were a knife thrust into her, and, turning awkwardly, runs out of the store.*]

VAL: You all better go or you'll get bogged down on th' road.

BLANCH: Dolly, you shouldn't have done that.

EVA: So unnecessary!

BEULAH: I don't know. She's always held herself so high.

DOLLY: Yes, superior to us all. I guess after this she won't have so much to say on the subjeck of bridge during Lent! Come on, Beulah, let's go! Blanch, you an' Eva comin'?

BLANCH: Yes, just a minute! What happened to those old shoes? You see 'em, Mr. Xavier?

VAL: I thrown 'em in the trash bin. You want 'em back?

BLANCH: Please.

EVA: We couldn't wear 'em, of course, but it's no use throwin' 'em away.

BLANCH: No. Willful waste makes woeful want, they say. [*She giggles as they back skittishly out of the door.*] Don't you feel it? The atmosphere is simply *charged* with electric disturbance! [*VAL is left alone. He picks up the canvas VEE left, places it on the counter and stares at it for several seconds. The CONJURE MAN comes back into the archway, gliding noiselessly as before. He stares inscrutably at VAL'S back. VAL turns, as MYRA had turned, with the same air of troubled presentiment, and catches the NEGRO'S gaze. Unconsciously he raises his hands to draw his shirt closer about his throat as though the air had turned colder.*]

VAL: What—what do you want? [*The CONJURE MAN mumbles almost indistinguishably.*] Oh. Sure. You can stay back there all night, if it don't stop raining! [*The CONJURE MAN grins and bows, then extends his palm with the lucky token.*] Huh? Naw, naw, naw, I don't want it! Sorry but I don't truck with that conjure stuff. [*The CONJURE MAN bows once more and disappears as noiselessly as he came. There is a low muttering of thunder. VAL looks uneasy. He takes off his working jacket. There is a wild burst of drunken laughter outside. The door is thrown open and SANDRA enters, a flash of lightning behind her. Her hair hangs loose and she wears a rain-spattered, grass-stained white satin evening gown.*]

SANDRA: Behold Cassandra, shouting doom at the gates!

VAL: What do you want?

SANDRA: Oh. It's you. Snakeskin. Remember we're even now.

VAL: What do you want in here?

SANDRA: Protection. I'm in danger.

VAL: Danger of what?

SANDRA: Immolation at the hands of the outraged citizens of Two Rivers County. They've confiscated the nigger that drove my car and ordered me out of Two Rivers.

VAL: You must've given 'em some provocation.

SANDRA: Plenty of provocation. They say that I run around wild and stir up trouble—and neither parental nor civil law is able to restrain me. Why, only this afternoon I was on Cypress Hill with that bright-skinned nigger. They suspect me of having improper relations with him.

VAL: Did you?

SANDRA: No. I poured a libation of rum on my great-aunt's grave. But they don't believe me. The Vigilantes decided that I was *persona non grata* and warned me to leave before something bad happened to me. How about you?

VAL: Huh?

SANDRA: Why don't you come along with me? You an' me, we belong to the fugitive kind. We live on motion. Think of it, Val. Nothing but motion, motion, mile after mile, keeping up with the wind, or even faster! Doesn't that make you hungry for what you live on? [VAL *shakes his head.*] Maybe we'll find something new, something never discovered. We'll stake out our claim before the others get to it. What do you say? [VAL *turns away.*] Where's Myra?

VAL: She's gone to Jackson Springs to get a doctor.

SANDRA: Good! We're alone together.

VAL: What's good about it?

SANDRA: Why do you hate me, Val?

VAL: I don't want trouble.

213

SANDRA: Am I trouble?

VAL: Yeah. As fine a piece of trouble as ever I've seen.

SANDRA: Is Myra trouble?

VAL: Leave her out of it.

SANDRA: Don't you think I know what's going on?

VAL: What are you talking about?

SANDRA: I saw her in Tupelo this morning, having her hair fixed up! What radiance! What joy!

VAL: Shut up about Myra.

SANDRA: Oh, you'd better watch out. It isn't kiss and good-bye with a woman like that! She'll want to keep you forever. I'm not like that.

VAL: Aw, leave me alone. [*He takes his jacket from a hook.*]

SANDRA: Women will never leave you alone. Not as long as you wear that marvelous jacket.

VAL: I want to close up.

SANDRA: I'll go in a minute.

VAL: Make it *this* minute, will you? [SANDRA *crosses to him. She loosens her red velvet cape and drops it to the floor at her feet. The white evening gown clings nakedly to her body.*]

VAL: Don't stand there in front of me like that!

SANDRA: Why not? I'm just looking at you. You know what I feel when I look at you, Val? Always the weight of your body bearing me down.

VAL: *Christ!*

214

SANDRA: You think I ought to be ashamed to say that? Well, I'm not. I think that passion is something to be proud of. It's the only one of the little alphabet blocks they give us to play with that seems to stand for anything of importance. Val . . . [*She touches his shoulder. He shoves her roughly away. The door opens and* MYRA *enters.*]

MYRA: Oh!

SANDRA [*casually*]: Hello, there. I thought you'd gone for the doctor.

MYRA: I couldn't get over the river. The bridge is out. What are *you* doing here?

SANDRA: I came here to give you a warning.

MYRA: A warning? Warning of what?

SANDRA: They've passed a law against passion. Our license has been revoked. We have to give it up or else be ostracized by Memphis society. Jackson and Vicksburg, too. Whoever has too much passion, we're going to be burned like witches because we know too much.

MYRA: What are you talking about?

SANDRA: Damnation! You see my lips have been touched by prophetic fire.

MYRA: I think they've also been touched by too much liquor. The store is closed.

SANDRA: I want to talk to you, Myra.

MYRA: Come back in the morning.

SANDRA: What morning? There isn't going to be any.

MYRA: I think there is.

SANDRA: That's just a case of unwarranted optimism. I have it on the very best of authority that time is all used up.

There's no more time. Can't you see it? Feel it? *[with drunken exultation]* The atmosphere is pregnant with disaster! *[She laughs and suddenly clasps the palms of her hands to her ears.]* Now, I can even *hear* it!

VAL: What?

SANDRA: A battle in heaven. A battle of *angels* above us! And *thunder!* And *storm! [She laughs wildly.]*

MYRA: Sandra, I've had too much. I can't stand anything more. You go home now before I do something I shouldn't.

SANDRA: I believe you *would*. You'd fight like a *tiger* for him.

MYRA: Be careful, Sandra.

SANDRA: Yes, I can tell by looking at you in that mad dress with your eyes spitting fire like the Devil's, you've learned what I've learned, that there's nothing on earth you can do. No, nothing! But catch at whatever comes near you with both your hands, until your fingers are broken! *[SANDRA flings herself upon VAL and kisses him with abandon. MYRA springs at her like a tiger and slaps her fiercely across the face.]*

MYRA: Leave him be, damn you, or I'll . . . *[SANDRA whimpers and staggers to the counter. Her head lolls forward and the dark hair slides over her face; she slips to her knees on the floor.]* Take her upstairs to my room. When dogs go mad, they ought to be locked and chained. *[VAL picks SANDRA up and carries her up the stairs. The storm increases in violence; rain beats loud on the tin portico outside. There is a terribly loud thunder clap. MYRA gasps. The electric current is disrupted and the lights dim out. Someone bangs at the door. MYRA calls—]* The store's closed up!

MAN: It's me, Mrs. Torrance. Jim Talbott!

MYRA: Oh, Sheriff Talbott. [*She opens the door.*] Is something the matter?

SHERIFF: Yes. [*He enters, followed by a woman. There is something remarkably sinister about the woman's appearance. She is a hard, dyed blond in a dark suit. Her body is short and heavy but her face appears to have been burned thin by some consuming fever accentuated by the masklike makeup she wears and the falsely glittering gems on her fingers which are knotted tight around her purse.*] This is Mrs. Regan from Waco, Texas.

WOMAN: Never mind about that. Where is the man that clerks here?

MYRA: Val?

WOMAN: Is that what he calls himself? In Waco he was known as Jonathan West.

MYRA [*to the* SHERIFF]: What does this woman want here?

WOMAN: I want that man.

SHERIFF: That clerk of yours is wanted for rape in Texas.

MYRA: I'm sure you're mistaken.

WOMAN: Oh, no, I don't think I am. I've sent out descriptions of him to every town in the country. Canada, Mexico, even. The minute I got news of this shoe clerk I hopped a plane out of Waco. I feel pretty sure that I've finally tracked him down. Where is he? Where does he keep himself?

MYRA: I don't know.

WOMAN: Surely you . . .

MYRA: I don't have any idea!

WOMAN: You—you *must*, Mrs. Torrance!

MYRA: *No!* No, I don't. Oh, yes, he—he drove into Memphis.

WOMAN: Two days before Easter? He suddenly drove into Memphis and left you without any help? That certainly does sound peculiar.

MYRA: I gave him his notice. He's gone.

WOMAN: I don't believe you.

MYRA [*to the* SHERIFF]: This woman has got a pistol in her purse.

WOMAN: What if I have? You don't go hunting a dangerous animal down without any weapons. [*She suddenly starts forward.*] Wait! Look here! This picture! [*She crosses to* VEE'S *portrait.*]

SHERIFF: It's one of my wife's.

WOMAN: Now I'm convinced. It's *him.* I'd recognize it hanging on the moon. Come along, Sheriff, we're wasting time with this woman. She's telling us lies to protect him. The place to look is them sporting houses on Front Street. [*She rushes from the store.*]

SHERIFF: Don't play with fire, Mrs. Torrance. [*He follows her out.* MYRA *gasps and crosses to the door, bolting it shut.* VAL *steps noiselessly out upon the upstairs landing and stares down at* MYRA. *He descends a few steps with caution.*]

VAL [*on the stairs*]: Who was it?

MYRA: Sheriff Talbott.

VAL [*descending two steps*]: Who was the woman? [MYRA *stares up at him dumbly.*] *Who was the woman with him?*

MYRA: Val, don't act so excited.

218

VAL: Oh. It was her then.

MYRA: Yes. The woman from Waco.

VAL: Christ! I heard her voice but I thought I must be dreaming. [*He suddenly catches his breath and darts down the stairs and toward the front door.*]

MYRA: Where do you think you're goin'?

VAL: *Out!*

MYRA: Don't be a fool. You can't leave now. Those drunken stave-mill workers are on the street.

VAL: They know, already? She's *told* 'em?

MYRA: Val, will you please . . .

VAL: Lock up that door!

MYRA: It's locked.

VAL: The door in the confectionery?

MYRA: That's locked, too.

VAL: What happened to the lights?

MYRA: Went out in the storm. I'll turn on a lamp . . .

VAL: No. *Don't!*

MYRA: In the confectionery. They can't see in.

VAL: What did you tell her?

MYRA: That you'd gone into Memphis.

VAL: Did she believe you?

MYRA: No.

VAL: Where did they go to look for me?

MYRA: Sporting houses on Front Street.

219

VAL: Yeah. She'd think of that. Oh, God, Myra, I've washed myself in melted snow on mountains trying to get the touch of her off my body. It's no good.

MYRA: Keep *hold* of yourself.

VAL: You can't understand what it is to be hounded by somebody's hate.

MYRA: I looked in her face. What I saw wasn't hate.

VAL: What was it then?

MYRA: A terrible, hopeless, twisted kind of *love.*

VAL: That's worse than hate.

MYRA: I *know.* [*She picks up a lamp.*] Dry as a bone. Give me the other one, Val. [VAL *stares at nothing.*] Never mind, I'll get it. You're safe in here. They looked here once; they won't come back until morning.

VAL: *Safe?* She mentioned it in her description.

MYRA: Mentioned what?

VAL: Scars from burns on his legs. Afraid of fire. She'll have them *burn* me, Myra.

MYRA: Oh, Val, darling, don't act like a scared little boy.

VAL: I'm not so scared. I'm sick.

MYRA: I know how you feel.

VAL: Like something was crawling on me. Something that crawled up out of the basement of my brain. How did she look?

MYRA: A vicious, pitiful, artificial blond.

VAL: She had on black?

MYRA: Yes.

VAL: All loaded down with imitation diamonds. That's how I see her. Leaning against a wall and screaming, "You can't get away! Anywhere that yuh go I'll track yuh down!" And now she has—She's *here!*

MYRA [*pityingly*]: Oh, Val, stay there on the stairs. I'm going to fix you a drink. The rain has made the air colder. Don't you feel it?

VAL: No.

MYRA: I do. I seem to be shaking a little. I guess my blood's too thin. Of course, you'll have to get away from Two River.

VAL: Get away? Yes, if I'm lucky!

MYRA: Oh, you'll be lucky, darling. I was just thinking, thinking about *myself*. Val . . .

VAL: What?

MYRA: I haven't traveled much. I've never been west of the Mississippi. Never much east of it either. I think it's time I took a trip somewhere.

VAL: What are you talking about?

MYRA: I'm leaving here with you tonight!

VAL: No.

MYRA: Oh, yes, I *am*. I've got to. We'll run off *together* as soon as the storm slacks up.

VAL [*rising*]: Myra . . .

MYRA: Give me a nickel; I want to play the victrola.

VAL: Myra, you're . . .

MYRA: No. Never mind. I've got some change in my pocket. Wait just a minute. [*She goes to the juke box and starts the music.*]

VAL: Myra, you've got to . . .

MYRA: *Shhh!* [*She comes back in.*] When I was a girl, I was always expecting something tremendous to happen. Maybe not this time but next time. I used to dance all night, come home drunk at daybreak and tiptoe barefooted up the back stairs. The sky used to be so white in the early mornings. You know it's been a long time since I've even noticed what color the sky is at daybreak. Traveling on a lonely road all night in an open car I guess you'd notice such things. I'd enjoy that. I could point them out to you while you were driving the car. I'd say, "Look, Val, here's something to put in the book!" "What is it?" I'd say, "It's white!" "What is?" "The sky is!" "Oh," you'd say, "is it?" "Yes," I'd say, "it is, it is, it *is!*" And you would have to believe me! [*She clings to him;* VAL *breaks away from her.*]

VAL: I got to go by myself. I couldn't take anyone with me.

MYRA: That's where you're mistaken. You're dreadfully mistaken if you think that I'm going to stay on here by myself in a store full of bottles and boxes while you go traipsing around through all the world's dark corners without me having a forwarding address even.

VAL: I'll give you a forwarding address.

MYRA: That's not enough. What could I do with a forwarding address, Val? Take it into the backroom with me at night? Oh, my darling, darling forwarding address! A wonderful companion *that* would be. So sweet. And satisfying!

VAL: Myra! Don't talk so loud!

MYRA [*breathlessly*]: Excuse me. I'll get your drink. [*She goes to the confectionery and comes back out with a bottle.*] How much do you want? Three fingers? What was I . . . ?

Oh, oh, yes, I wanted to tell you [*she pours the rum*] we had a fig tree in the back of our yard that never bore any fruit. We thought that it never would. I'd always pitied it so because they said it was barren. But it surprised us one spring. I was the one that discovered the first little fig. Oh, my God, I was so excited. I ran in the house; I was screaming, "Daddy, daddy, it isn't barren, it isn't barren, daddy! The little fig tree . . ." I told him, "It's going to have figs this year!" It seemed such a marvelous thing, it needed a big celebration, so I took out Christmas ornaments. Yes, little colored glass bells and tinsel and artificial snow! [*She laughs breathlessly.*] And I put them all over the fig tree, there, in the middle of April, because it was going to bear fruit! Here, Val, step up to the bar and take your drink! [VAL *crosses to her*] Oh, darling, haven't we any Christmas ornaments to hang on me? [VAL *stops short.*]

VAL [*sharply*]: What do you mean?

MYRA: I mean that I'm not barren. Not anymore!

VAL: You're making this up!

MYRA: No, Val! You see, being clever, Val, isn't enough when you're up against something as big as life is. Sure, you can make keys for a door. That's clever, Val, but somebody comes along and breaks the door down. That's life! And that's what happened to me. Oh, God, I knew that I wouldn't be barren when we went together that first time. I felt it already, stirring up inside me, beginning to live! The first little fig on the tree they said wouldn't bear. What a mistake they made! Here. Here's your drink. [*He stares at her dumbly.*] Take it! [*She thrusts it into his hand.*] So now you see we can't be separated! We're bound together, Val!

VAL: Bound? No! I'm not bound to nothing! Never could be, Myra!

223

MYRA: Oh, yes, you could!

VAL: What do you mean by that?

MYRA: In one respect I'm like that woman from Waco. I'll never let you get away from me, Val. I want you to understand that.

VAL: There's one thing you don't understand good, Myra.

MYRA: No? What's that?

VAL: I travel by myself. I don't take anything with me but my skin.

MYRA: Then I'm your skin. Skin yourself and you'll be rid of me!

VAL: Listen, Myra, there's one thing safe for me to do. Go back to New Mexico and live by myself.

MYRA: On the desert?

VAL: Yes.

MYRA: Would I make the desert crowded?

VAL: Yes, you would. You'd make it crowded, Myra.

MYRA: Oh, my God, I thought a desert was *big.*

VAL: It is big, Myra. It stretches clean out 'til tomorrow. Over here is the Labos Mountains, and over there, that's Sangre de Cristo. And way up there, that's the sky! And there ain't nothing else in between, not you, not anybody, or nothing.

MYRA: I see.

VAL: Why, my God, it seems like sometimes when you're out there alone by yourself (not with nobody else!) that your brain is stretched out so far, it's pushing right up against the edges of the stars!

MYRA: Uh, huh! Maybe, that's what happened! [*She laughs harshly.*] That's why you act so peculiar; you scrambled your brains on the stars so you can't think straight!

VAL: Shut up, God damn you!

MYRA: Val! [*Rain falls in a gust on the tin portico. There is a silence between them.*]

VAL: I'm sorry, Myra.

MYRA: So what are you planning to do? Drive west by yourself?

VAL: Yes. [*He moves to the wall and takes his book out.*]

MYRA: You can't leave yet. Those stave-mill workers are still across the street.

VAL: In two or three more years she may forget . . .

MYRA: The woman from Waco?

VAL: Yes.

MYRA: I don't think so. I don't think she ever will.

VAL: Well, anyway, when I've finished this book I'm going to send for you.

MYRA: Are you? Why?

VAL: Because I do love you, Myra.

MYRA: Love? You're too selfish for love. You're just like a well full of water without any rope, without any bucket, without any tin cup even. God pity the fool that comes to you with a dry tongue!

VAL: I promise I'll send for you, Myra.

MYRA: Thanks. Thanks. And what'll I do in the mean-time? Stay on here with our lucky little. . . . What shall I call

it? Myra's little Miracle from Heaven? [*She laughs wildly.*
JABE *knocks on the ceiling.*]

VAL: Jabe's knocking.

MYRA: Don't you think that I hear him? Knock, knock,
knock! It sounds like bones, like death, and that's what it is.
Ask me how it feels to be coupled with death up there. His
face was always so thin, so yellow, so drawn. I swear to you,
Val, his face on the pillow at night, it resembled a skull. He
wore a nightshirt like a shroud, and when he got up in the
dark, you know what I said to myself? "It's walking," I said
to myself, "the ghost is walking!" And I—I had to endure
him! Ahh, my flesh always crawled when he touched me.
Yes, but I stood it, though. I guess I knew in my heart that
it wouldn't go on forever, the way I suppose the fig tree knew
in spite of those ten useless springs it wouldn't be barren
always. When you come in off the road and asked for a job,
I said to myself "This is it, this is what you been waiting for,
Myra!" So I said with my eyes, "Stay here, stay here, for the
love of God, stay here." And you did, you stayed. And just
about at that time, as though for that special purpose, he
started dying upstairs, when I started coming to life. It was
like a battle had gone on between us those ten years, and I,
the living, had beaten him, the dead one, back to the grave
he climbed out of! Oh, for a while I tried to fight myself but
it was no use. It was like I was standing down there at the
foot of the levee and watched it break and known it was no
use running. I tried to get rid of the key but that didn't work.
Since then all decency's left me, I've stood like a woman
naked with nothing but love—love, love. [*She clings to him
fiercely.*]

VAL: Let go of me, Myra. [*He shoves her roughly away.*]
You're like the woman from Waco. The way you . . .

MYRA [*slowly*]: You know what I've done? I've smashed myself against a rock. [*She crosses to the door.*] If you try to leave here without me, I'll call for the Sheriff!

VAL: That's what she did.

MYRA: *I'll* do it, *too.* Strike me in the face so I can scream. [*She catches at him again, he breaks loose, she utters a choked cry. The door slams open on the landing. At this instant a flickering match light appears on the stairs and spills down them and across the floor. Heavy dragging footsteps and hoarse breathing are heard.*]

MYRA [*whispering*]: Christ in Heaven, what's that? [*The ghastly, phantom-like effect of this entrance is dramatically underlined.* JABE'S *shadow precedes him down the stairs and his approach has the slow, clumping fatality of the traditional spook's. He is a living symbol of death, as* MYRA *has described him. He wears a purple bathrobe which hangs shroudlike about his figure and his face is a virtual death mask. Just as he appears in full view in the stairwell, the match which he holds under his face flickers out and disappears from view, swallowed in darkness like a vanished apparition.*]

MYRA [*horrified, incredulous*]: Jabe.

JABE [*hoarsely*]: Yes, it's me! [*He strikes another match and this time his face wears a grotesque, grinning expression.*] I didn't have much luck at knocking on the floor.

MYRA [*dazed*]: I didn't hear you.

JABE: Naw?

MYRA: The storm made too much noise.

JABE: Aw, absorbed in the storm.

MYRA: Yes.

JABE: Lamp light, huh?

MYRA: Yes, the lights went out when that awful lightning struck.

JABE: Your dress is torn open.

MYRA: You did that, Jabe, when I tried to give you morphine.

JABE: I thought you might give me too much.

MYRA: How did you get out of bed?

JABE: The usual way. Why? Does that seem remarkable to you?

MYRA: Yes. I didn't know you was able to.

JABE: You always been too optimistic about my condition. [MYRA *gasps involuntarily with loathing.* JABE *laughs hoarsely.*] I'm okay now. I'm not going to cash my chips in yet for a while. [VAL *coughs uneasily and clears his throat.*]

MYRA: Jabe—Jabe, this is Val Xavier.

JABE: You don't need to introduce me. I know him; I'm payin' his wages. [*To* VAL:] Myra here seems to think I had a tumor on the brain and they cut the brain out an' left the tumor. [*He laughs again and Myra repeats her involuntary gasp of loathing.*] Gimme that lamp; I wanta look at the stock.

MYRA: Here. We finished straightening up.

JABE: Aw, is that what you was doing?

MYRA: Yes. Val couldn't go home in the storm so we took advantage of the extra time.

JABE: Uh-huh. [*He takes the candle and goes unsteadily toward the confectionery. He passes through the archway;*

the pale walls hung with artificial blossoms have an eery effect in candlelight. The confectionery has a misty, flickering unreal pallor like a region of death, and JABE, *in his long dark robe, stands at the entrance like the very Prince of Darkness. He hesitates as though he senses that deathlike quality himself.*] Hell. It looks like a goddam honky-tonk since you done it over! [*He moves resolutely on into the room.*]

MYRA [*under her breath*]: Oh, God, I can't stand it, Val. I'm going to scream! Say something to him. Don't stand there doing nothing!

VAL: What should I say to him?

MYRA: Oh, I don't know—anything! [*She speaks in a loud, false tone.*] It seems miraculous, don't it, to see him downstairs?

VAL [*uncertainly*]: Yes. [JABE *laughs mockingly in the next room. Very softly:*] Death's in the orchard, Myra!

MYRA: Val.

JABE: How about a little pinball game? Would you like to play one, Mr. Whatsit?

MYRA: Answer him!

VAL [*inaudibly*]: No.

JABE: Huh? Can't you talk out loud in there?

VAL [*shouting*]: No! No!

MYRA: Shhh!

JABE: I think I'll shoot a few.

VAL: Give me my wages. Let me get out. [VAL *moves towards the counter, but* MYRA *blocks him.*]

MYRA: You can't leave me alone with him, would you?

JABE: Hot damn. I clicked on three.

MYRA: You couldn't be such a coward.

VAL: Let go of my arm.

JABE: Twenty-five hundred, Myra.

VAL: This place is shrinking; the walls are closing in!

JABE: Thirty-five. Forty-five.

MYRA: Give me time, darling. A little more time. [VAL *tears loose.*]

JABE: Fifty!

MYRA: I swear to God, I won't let you.

JABE: Right down the middle aisle, twice straight.

VAL: Let go!

JABE: Sixty-five, seventy.

MYRA: You've got to stick with me, Val.

VAL: Don't have to do nothing. I'm going!

JABE: Buzzards! Buzzards!!!! I hear you croaking in there. You think you've got a corpse to feed on, but you ain't! I'm going to live, Myra. [MYRA'S *hysteria is released. She laughs wildly and rushes to the doorway.*]

MYRA: Oh, no, you're not; no, you're not! You're going to die, Jabe. You're rotten with death already!

JABE [*shouting*]: Die, am I?

MYRA: Yes, and I'm glad, I'm *glad,* I'm planning a celebration! I'm going to wear Christmas ornaments in my hair!

Why? Because I'm not barren. I've gotten death out of me and now I've taken life in! Yes, oh, yes, I've got *life* in me— in *here! [She clasps her hands over her stomach.]* Do you see what I've got my hands on? Well, that's where it *is,* you see! I'm way, way, way up *high!* And you can't drag me *down!* Not any more, Mr. *Death!* We're through with each other. *[She laughs in wild exultance; then suddenly covers her face and runs sobbing back to* VAL. *She is terrified.]* Val! *[She clutches his arm. He breaks away and crosses toward the front door of the store.]*

VAL: It's finished! *[He goes to the cash register, rings it open.* JABE *creeps in with the lantern, unseen by them, and steals towards the hardware counter.]*

MYRA *[screaming at him wildly, completely distracted]:* What are you doing? You're robbing the store!

VAL: I'm taking my wages out.

MYRA: You're robbing the store; I won't let you! *[She rushes to the phone and shouts into it.* JABE *is loading a revolver.]* Give me the Sheriff's house. The store's being robbed!

VAL: Go on, you little bitch.

MYRA: The store's being robbed, the clerk is robbing the store. He's running off with the money; you got to stop him! *[*JABE'S *face is livid with hatred and he holds the revolver, which he levels carefully at* MYRA, *holding the candle above him to give a light.]*

JABE: Buzzards! *[He fires. The first shot strikes* MYRA. *She utters a smothered cry and clutches at the wall.* VAL *springs at him and wrests the revolver from his grasp.]*

VAL: You shot her.

JABE [*slowly, panting*]: Naw. *You* shot her. Didn'tja hear her shouting your name on the phone? She said you was robbing the store! They'll come here an' burn you for it! Buzzards! [*He turns slowly and staggers out the front door. His voice is heard shouting wildly against the wind.* VAL *gasps, slams the door, and bolts it, the revolver still in his grasp.* MYRA *moves out from the shadow of the wall with a slight, sobbing breath.*]

VAL: Myra! You're hurt!

MYRA: Yes.

VAL: How bad?

MYRA: I don't know. I don't feel nothing at all. It struck me here, where I would have carried the child. There's nothing but death in me now.

VAL: I'll call for the doctor!

MYRA: There's no way to get any doctor. Go on, look out for yourself, get away! I don't need anyone now. . . . [*She staggers out from the wall.*] Isn't it funny that I should just now remember what happened to the fig tree? It was struck down in a storm, the very spring that I hung those ornaments on it. Why? Why? For what reason? Because some things are enemies of light and there is a battle between them in which some fall! [*The confectionery suddenly blooms into soft springlike radiance as the electric current resumes.*] Oh, look! The lights have come on in the confectionery! [*She staggers through the archway.*] That's what I wanted! Not death, but David—the orchard across from Moon Lake! [*She advances a few more steps and disappears from sight. Her body is heard falling.* VAL *crosses to the archway.*]

VAL: Myra! Myra! [*The lights flicker and go out. Now the clamor of the crowd is heard distantly. Under his breath:*]

Fire! [*He looks frenziedly about him for a moment, then plunges out through the confectionery. A door opens at the top of the stairs and* SANDRA *appears, aroused by the clamor. At first she descends the steps fearfully, then with a sort of exultation, appearing like a priestess in her long, sculptural white dress. When she has reached the bottom of the stairs, the front door is opened and the* WOMAN FROM WACO *enters, the crowd crying out behind her and the pine torches glaring through the windows.*]

WOMAN [*to* SANDRA]: You—where is he?

SHERIFF: Watch out, Mrs. Regan! He's armed!

MRS. REGAN: So am I! Where is he?

SHERIFF [*advancing not too bravely*]: Xavier! [*A flickering light appears in the confectionery.*]

MAN: In back!

VOICES: In the confectionery! Get him! Git him outta there! Kill him! Burn the son of a bitch! Burn him!

WOMAN FROM WACO: What are you waiting fo'? Scared—scared? [*She plunges toward the archway with drawn revolver. The* CONJURE MAN *suddenly appears, hearing a lantern. The shocking apparitional effect of his entrance stuns them for a second. The* WOMAN FROM WACO *stops short with a stifled cry.*]

VOICE: Christ! Who's that? The Conjure Man! The Conjure Man from Blue Mountain!

WOMAN: Git out of my way! Make him git outta my way!

SHERIFF [*stepping up beside her*]: Where is Xavier, you niggah? [*Slowly, tremblingly, the* NEGRO *elevates something in his hand. He holds it above his head. There is a momentary hush as all eyes are centered upon this lividly mottled*

233

object, which, though inanimate, still keeps about it the hard, immaculate challenge of things untamed.]

A VOICE: His jacket!

ANOTHER: *The Snakeskin Jacket!* [*The* WOMAN FROM WACO *screams and covers her face. A gong is struck and the stage is drowned in instant and utter blackness.*]

CURTAIN

EPILOGUE

*After a few seconds the curtain is raised again, and we are
returned to the Sunday afternoon a year later. The scene
is the same as for the Prologue. The stage is empty and
sinister with its testimony of past violence. Faintly, as from
some distance, there comes the sound of chanting from a
Negro church. The store itself is like a pillaged temple with
the late afternoon sunlight thrown obliquely through the high
Gothic windows in the wall at the left. The* CONJURE MAN
*sits with immobile dignity upon his stool near the archway
like the Spirit of the Dead Watching. The door at the top
of the stairs opens and the* TEMPLE SISTERS *emerge with
their customers.*

BLANCH: Watch out for these stairs; they're awful, awful
steep! Eva, you better go first with the lamp.

EVA [*descending first*]: Uncle! Uncle!

BLANCH: He's deaf as a post! [*The* CONJURE MAN *rises.*]

EVA: Oh, there you are, Uncle. Bring us Cassandra's things
from that shelf over there. [*The* CONJURE MAN *complies with
slow dignity.*]

BLANCH: We only have two things that belonged to Cassandra Whiteside on display in the museum.

EVA [*displaying the articles*]: This pair of dark sunglasses
and this bright red cape.

BLANCH: Cassandra's body was never recovered from the
Sunflower River.

EVA: Some people say that she didn't know the bridge was
washed out.

235

BLANCH: But we know better, however. She deliberately drove her car into the river and drowned because she knew that *decent* people were done with her.

EVA: Absolutely. The Vigilantes had warned her to get out of town.

BLANCH: Now, Uncle, the *Snakeskin Jacket*.

EVA: He's already got it.

BLANCH: That is one article in the museum that me an' Eva won't lay our bare hands on.

EVA: I don't know what, but it simply terrifies me.

BLANCH: Uncle, hold it up there in the archway like you did when you reported his capture. [*The* CONJURE MAN *unfolds the jacket which he had held in his lap and elevates it above his head as he did at the end of the preceding scene.*]

EVA: It's marvelous how fresh and clean it stays.

BLANCH: Other things get dusty. But not the jacket. What was it that Memphis newspaper-woman called it? "A souvenir of the jungle!"

EVA: "A shameless, flaunting symbol of the Beast Untamed!"

BLANCH: Put it down, Uncle. Uncle was washing the car in back of the store when the murderer tried to escape by that back door.

EVA: He fell right in the hands of the stave-mill workers.

BLANCH: They torn off his clothes an' thrown him into a car.

EVA: Drove him right down the road to the lynching tree . . .

BLANCH: That big cottonwood where the road turned off toward th' levee.

EVA: Exackly where Vee Talbott seen him that day in her vision.

BLANCH: We showed you the Jesus picture? That was the last thing she painted before she lost her mind.

EVA: Which makes five lives, as they said in one of the papers . . .

BLANCH: "Tied together in one fatal knot of passion."

EVA: Not counting the woman from Waco, who disappeared.

BLANCH: Nobody knows what ever become of her. [*She crosses to the wall and takes something down.*]

EVA [*with relish*]: Oh, the blow-tawch!

BLANCH: It's not the original one but it's one just like it. Look! [*She presses a valve and a fierce blue jet of flame stabs into the dark atmosphere. The woman tourist utters a sharp, involuntary cry and sways slightly forward, covering her eyes.*]

WOMAN: Oliver, take me out! [*The man hastily assists her to the door.*]

BLANCH [*to* EVA]: They haven't paid yet!

EVA: *Fifty cents, please! That will be fifty cents!*

BLANCH: To keep up the museum!

EVA: Yes, to preserve the memorial—twenty-five cents each.

[*They go out, following the tourists. The door remains open. Sunlight flows serenely, warmly, through it, a golden contradiction of all that is past. The* CONJURE MAN *glides toward the door. His face assumes a venomous, mocking*

237

look. He crouches forward, and spits out the open door with dry crackling laughter, then turns, and, unfolding the brilliant snakeskin jacket once more, he goes to the back wall and hangs it above his head in the shaft of sunlight through the door. He seems to make a slight obesiance before it. The religious chant from across the wide cotton fields now swells in exaltation as the curtain falls.]